OUTSPOKEN

Clarence W. Newsome, Esq.

A CIVIL RIGHTS CHAMPION

A Daughter's Reflections

DR. CLARENCIA NEWSOME-SHADE

Printed in the United States of America

2020 First Edition

10 9 8 7 6 5 4 3 2 1

Subject Index:

Newsome-Shade, Clarencia Dr.

Title: Outspoken: A Civil Rights Champion, Clarence W. Newsome: A Daughter's Reflections

1. Civil Rights Movement 2. The Richmond 34 3. U.S. Race Relations 4. African-American Families 5. Virginia Union University 6. Howard University School of Law 7. Daughter's Biography 8. Oliver W. Hill 9. Henry L. Marsh III 10. L. Douglas Wilder 11. Justice Thurgood Marshall

Library of Congress Card Catalog Number: 2020901140

Paperback ISBN: 978-0-578-63808-9

New Some Legacy Publishing LLC

outspokenlawyer.com

PRAISES FOR OUTSPOKEN...

"The idea of a marvelous life-altering discovery is intriguing because it hardly ever occurs for most people. After a successful career as a Psychologist and Supervisor in Urban Education, Dr. Clarencia Shade lost her beloved mother and subsequently began a quest to learn about the biological father she barely knew due to her parents' divorce and his early death. Her dedicated search led to this inspirational and compelling story of her exceptional father's career, and the quest for education and purpose that binds together both sides of this exceptional African American family. Dr. Shade's book entrances with a story that allows us to vicariously experience her personal journey, and a reminder of the undeniable influence of genes."

Cheryl LuSane, School Administrator,
Newark Public Schools and Department
of Defense Education Activity

"It is my pleasure to endorse this wonderful piece of history, *Outspoken, Clarence W. Newsome, Esq. A Civil Rights Champion: A Daughter's Reflections,* by my friend and fellow yoke bearer, Clarencia Newsome-Shade. Mr. Newsome, a historical icon shared information that every Black American and lover of our history should revere. His legal mind and career make us proud to be Black, educated and compassionate in an America filled with strife, inequality, and injustice. It was my pleasure to teach vocal music in the Plainfield Public School District for nearly 30 years. Although music was the focal point, I did my best to share our history and to create a yearning for this knowledge.

Each year we celebrated Kwanzaa, Black History Month and gained a greater respect for Kwanzaa's 7 principles.

This book should be in every library that teaches our history. In addition, the mission statement of my choir, Jubilation, includes educating the community regarding our history and rich heritage. Again, this book is a must for every member, as we strive to permeate our surroundings with the greatness of Black Americans. I applaud Clare for her strength in sharing this wonderful work which informs the public of tremendous historical accounts. Her courage is commendable. To GOD be the glory for the great things we do and witness!"

The Rev. Stefanie R. Minatee, DMin.
Artistic Director
"Transforming the World Through Education and Music Ministry, One Song at a Time..."
www.jubilationchoir.org

"Hail to Dr. Shade for bringing this civil rights titan to the forefront of our collective consciousness in this compelling biography. Clarence W. Newsome's obscurity does not match the enormity of his contributions to the cause of eradicating racial segregation and injustice. Her treatment of the Richmond 34 case is particularly riveting. Yet, there's even more to this book than this civil rights pioneer's gallant fight for racial justice, for there is also the personal side of a daughter chronicling the life of her father, and in doing so, connecting with him, which even further elevates the significance of the the telling of this story."

Anthony R. Gartmond, Esq., Retired Assistant Prosecutor, Essex County Prosecutor's Office

DEDICATION

To my children, Leon and Sharm, and my grandchildren Leah, Rick Jr., Effie, and Jayden. To my parents Dr. Cora Jeffries-Duncan, Deacon Alfonso Duncan, my sister Rev. Dr. Imani-Sheila Newsome Camara, and to my father, Clarence W. Newsome. To all those front-line and behind the scenes, heroes, and sheroes who worked tirelessly for justice and equality for Black Americans during the Jim Crow Era and beyond. Hold on. Faint not as the struggle continues...

"The imprint of a father remains forever on the life of a child."

- Roy Lessin

TABLE OF CONTENTS

FOREWORD

I t is harmful to live with ghosts. They linger in the shadows nibbling away at the clarity of our lives. We must bring them out of the shadows and into the light of life. We must give them flesh and blood, turning them into allies for well-being rather than thieves who rob us of crucial information.

So, we must resurrect the dead, especially of those we love. We resurrect our loved ones so we can rehearse the impact they had on our lives. As we dwell with them and the memories they invoke, we understand that they lived before us, they lived with us, and they live in us. Then, as allies, they give us lives to reflect upon and impart those lessons to others.

I admit I was comfortable with the ghost of our father, Clarence William Newsome, Esquire. Not all ghosts are scary. He was allowed to flicker around the edges of my life. I knew he was handsome, smart, and dedicated to helping others. I gained more respect for the Newsome name as I looked through my father's old yearbook at Virginia Union University in Richmond, Virginia, when I studied there or mentioned his name in that city. Any mention of his name was met with high regard and praise. I felt close to the shadow of the man, and that was enough. Still, the little I knew of him I held with pride never relinquishing fragments of his story or his last name. With the acquisition of my B.S. degree from Virginia Union, every scholarship, award, degree, and professional title I obtained in Education, and Theological Studies, I paid homage to my father's ghost.

On the other hand, my sister, Rev. Dr. Clarencia Rene Shade, is the ghost hunter. Our father, Clarence William Newsome, Esquire, with his divorce from our mother, Dr. Cora F. Duncan, his relocation to the south, and his death, May 24, 1963, was a ghost to both my sister and me. After looking in an old suitcase that held pictures, yearbooks, and documents about our father, Clarencia had the courage to bring our father into the light of life. Methodically, she began to look back over our father's life beyond the photographs and documents she found. Over the years, while making her climb to excellence as an agent of healing and justice as a renowned therapist and leader, she devoted time to research. She called libraries, explored archives, dug up family roots, made telephone calls, sent emails and texts, ultimately piecing together an image of a man neither of us had known. The result of all that work and unnamed sacrifices is the recreated legacy of our father, Clarence William Newsome, Esquire in this book, *Outspoken*.

This book is also about the life of my sister Clarencia. Our entire family, especially her children Leon and Sharmonique, their children, and her niece, Mariama, will learn about the power of overcoming. In it, readers will find vignettes about the complexities of love, family building, and resilience, as exhibited in her life. I also view this work as a gift to me. My story is woven into her story, and I thank my sister for that. She has recorded conversations I never participated in with my mother, stories I cannot tell, memories I do not have, and a few I do. However, I do remember the words that came from my stepdad about my father. I am blessed by Clarencia's focus on familial stories that still have an impact on my life. Finally, this book about my father inspires me to continue my work as a Christian theologian and minister who cares for others. All my work that emerges from years of teaching in undergraduate and graduate programs, as well as a major seminary, has been undergirded by my father's legacy of civil rights and justice work.

Outspoken is a breakthrough book that follows the work of historians of the modern Civil Rights Era who have recovered the life stories of women, men, and children who gave the Movement its momentum. There is so much of this work yet to be done by family members, community members, colleagues, and scholars. Perhaps this book will inspire others to begin researching and writing similar books.

The legacy Rev. Dr. Shade uncovers is not only for me, our family or in service to modern Civil Rights Era scholarship. I hope others use her work as a blueprint for those who are steering through the continuing maze of work attached to advocacy for civil and human rights in a complex global community in the twenty-first century. *Outspoken* offers a glimpse of the power of vocation and voice in service to justice for those who are in the process of discovering both. Well done, sister. Thank you for paving the way for our father's legacy to live on for generations.

Rev. Dr. Imani-Sheila Newsome-Camara
Christian Theologian
Pastor-Teacher
Greenwood Memorial United Methodist Church,
Boston, Massachusetts

ACKNOWLEDGMENTS

I want to thank Peter Wallenstein, who helped me begin my contoured silhouette of my father, satisfying the craving for more than a photograph. His book, *Blue Laws, Black Code,* is the first internet reference that appeared in my online searches in 2013 which helped me tremendously. I would also like to thank the City of Richmond and the Department of Historic Resources responsible for the application and inventory of the Jackson-Ward buildings to become a part of the National Register of Historic Places which lists my father's home as a historic landmark.

Thanks to Dr. Raymond Pierre Hylton for including my father in his book and incorporating my father into the 60th celebration of The Richmond 34. To Magaret Edds, author of *We Face the Dawn,* for pointing me in the right direction to research certain archives.

I am also indebted to Governor L. Douglas Wilder, who documented serving as my father's campaign councilman in his book, *Native Son of Virginia.* Also, to the authors, researchers, and journalists of the Afro-American Newspaper and countless journalists who reported the facts in newspapers, magazines and preserved in library archives in the

Richmond, Virginia libraries, and the librarians in Roanoke, Virginia.

To my new found family members, Kimberley, Joseph, and Calvin, with whom I am recently acquainted. Finally, I would like to thank my book coach Kim Rouse, The Painless Book Coach,™ who gave this project both her expertise and her heart. I could not have completed this work without you.

INTRODUCTION

"My father was a champion of the Civil Rights Era, a rebel, and a bright young lawyer. Nearly sixty years later, discovering his legacy has helped me find my missing 'peace'."

- Clarencia Newsome-Shade

Losing a parent through death, divorce, or a break-up at a young age or any age can be devastating. My father died in 1963 when I was six years old. For me, the emotional trauma began to emerge when I realized that I had zero recollection of my father—his voice, his smell, his touch, or his physical appearance. Childhood trauma is an "experience of an event by a child that is emotionally painful or distressful, which often results in lasting mental and physical effects."[1] Children are unable to comprehend death due to a common psychological child development term called "magical thinking." Magical thinking kicks in when events or concepts are beyond a child's comprehension, so they create theories as a defense mechanism against fear of the unknown.

My father met my mother when they were both in graduate school at Howard University in Washington, D.C. He was a law student, and she was in the postgraduate social work program. My parents separated, divorced, and remarried when I was two years old, and my sister Sheila was five. So, our stepfather, Alfonso Duncan, was the only dad that we knew and loved. Daddy Duncan was a wonderful father in every way imaginable, but for me, knowing that he was not my *real* dad, left a silent, piercing void that has finally been filled.

Completing this book has not been an easy feat. The emotional roller coaster I faced caused me to start and stop over and over again for decades. Sometimes I had this feeling of anticipation as when a roller coaster climbs the first steep incline, trying to determine how to brace myself for the fall. I never knew what to expect in my search. Other times I had this fear, and my stomach was in knots like when the roller coaster makes that first drop.

Asking my mother about my father was usually met with tension. I was not allowed to be outspoken about this matter whenever the mood struck. Adults during my mother's generation were secretive and private. The prevailing school of thought was to "stay out of grown folks business" and to be seen but not heard. Although she gave me minor bits and pieces of information, my mother reasoned that my line of questioning was, "Rubbing her nose in the past." My mom repeated a carefully crafted narrative to me about my father's brilliance, drinking, and socialite ways. I am convinced that she genuinely believed her version. To be honest, I finally had the confidence to pursue publishing my father's story after her transition in 2017. I miss her dearly, but I know she will be proud of the result.

It wasn't until I became a teenager that I started to show signs of moodiness and depression. Adolescence is a growth stage where identity is at the top of the list for budding young adults. My identity emerged as triangulated between my step-up father, my mysterious biological father that I never knew, and my mother, a college-educated powerhouse in her own right. On occasion, she would utter that I was like my father, "a brilliant lawyer." Yet, the cloak of secrecy about him remained. I didn't know whether to be happy or sad, proud, or ashamed. I just learned to live with the complexity of my tripartite identity.

As a young person, it never occurred to me to go to the library to search for newspaper articles about my father. History was being written while I was growing up. The Civil Rights Era was unfolding in front of our eyes on TV, in the newspapers, and everyday life experiences. Living in the northeast also meant that I did not directly encounter Jim Crow Laws as a child or young adult. I did not understand the Movement, nor could I have imagined that my father was playing a role in it. My parents were careful to shield my older sister and me from the negativity that surrounded prejudices against Blacks.

When we traveled, we only frequented places that were accommodating to Blacks. Daddy Duncan would take a long way home to prevent eyewitness accounts of poverty, homelessness, or the "projects or bricks" if you lived in neighboring towns like Newark. On road trips, we used Triple-A and the actual "Negro Motorist Greenbook" like in the movie, to study maps and make sure we were on safe routes for Blacks. The Greenbook highlighted which towns were "sundown towns" or "sunset towns" which vehemently upheld segregation and enforced restrictions on all non-whites traveling through those towns. Many of these towns had signs posted in their city, which read, "Nigger, Don't Let the Sun Go Down on You in _____." This was scary for me as a little girl. Daddy Duncan loved maps, and my mother loved to travel so we were on the road often. Our family trips were memorable, and mom always made sure we had fried chicken or turkey sandwiches with mayonnaise in a picnic basket, slices of pound cake, and cold drinks in our thermos.

In 2017, I finally got serious and began researching my father's life and impact during the Civil Rights Movement in Richmond, Virginia. I went to the Richmond and Roanoke libraries to begin my quest. During this journey, I researched thousands of pages of information in magazines, newspapers, journals, obituaries, books, and interviews with relatives to finally create my personal sketch of a living, breathing pioneer for justice and equality for Black people—my people.

Before my research, everything I had learned about the Civil Rights Movement involved Dr. Martin Luther King Jr., Rosa Parks, and the Montgomery Bus Boycott. I was aware of the Jim Crow Laws in the South, and other significant contributions made by Black inventors, and other famous activists for the struggle, during my middle school years for Black History

Month. My knowledge and exposure were limited. Yet, as I began to uncover facts and information deeper than the nutshell summaries, I acquired a more intimate connection to the 20th Century Black America struggle, that unfortunately mirrors the Black struggle today.

The early Civil Rights Movement in Richmond, Virginia, set the tone for the rest of the Southern states. The heroes and sheroes were the Black lawyers who beat the system by applying its own rules to an unequal system created by white legislators and the powers that be. My father won Fourteenth Amendment victories for his clients in interstate travel, desegregation of public libraries, schools, unjustified arrests at social clubs, and other public places. He fought for compulsory attendance law to avoid high schoolers dropping out, as well as fair wages for Black teachers. He won several personal injury lawsuits and settled high-profile cases and was part of the NAACP legal defense team.

My father was directly involved in the noteworthy Richmond 34 case, where a group of students from Virginia Union University participated in nonviolent sit-ins at Thalhimers Department Store, as well as the interstate travel case of Boynton, a Freedom Rider, from Howard University. Both cases went all the way to the United States Supreme Court. His work paved the way for the election of the first Black Mayor of Richmond, Henry L. Marsh III, and the first Black governor of Virginia, L. Douglas Wilder, both good friends of my father and legal colleagues. My father was present in meetings and planning sessions with Dr. Martin Luther King, Jr. He also helped free

Reverend Wyatt Tee Walker from jail when Walker led the protest against segregated libraries in St. Petersburg, Virginia. I am incredibly proud to say that my father, Clarence Newsome, is no longer my past—he's my present.

Quite frankly, I am honored to see my father's name chronicled in several 50th Anniversary books about The Civil Rights Movement. I get goosebumps, and the tiny hairs stand up on the back of my neck when I read, "Clarence W. Newsome was a front-line roleplayer in dismantling injustices including Jim Crow Laws, school segregation, and countless other Black discrimination incidents that occurred in the south."[2]

While many people celebrate the achievements and sacrifices of The Movement in the 1960s, I now personally celebrate the recognition and the archived documentation of my father's courage and outspokenness to fight for Black equality in this country. Although many narratives about landmark cases lump his contributions together as a member of a legal team, I discovered that he was a front-line defense attorney of the famous law firm of the South, Hill, Tucker, Olphin, and Marsh. My father prepared the briefs, filed the petitions, argued publicly, and in courtrooms for justice. The Hill firm filed and won more civil rights cases than any of the Southern states combined. The firm's historical role was a significant catalyst in the Movement. Before my father's hiring, the Hill firm won the *Brown vs. Board of Education* cases. My father was also part of the NAACPlegal defense team and traveled across the country representing Black injustices and discrimination.

I believe that had my father lived longer, he too would have been a household name like his famous colleagues. Especially in light of the careers of L. Douglas Wilder, who became a member of the Senate and the first Black governor of Virginia, or Henry L. Marsh III, the first Black Mayor of Richmond, Virginia. Not to mention, Oliver Hill, who received a Presidential Medal of Honor for his legal acumen fighting for civil rights. Who knows, maybe he would have become a United States Supreme Court appointee like Thurgood Marshall? All of these great men of The Movement were older than my father and were his friends, brothers, and graduates from Howard University School of Law.

The more I learned of his characteristics, mannerisms, and features, his reflection and impact on my being are undeniable. My cousin Kim pointed out that my son is the spitting image of my father minus the dimples. It's uncanny to see my son make facial expressions that look identical to his grandfather from the newspaper photos. I have a new respect for genetics.

My mother always pointed out how I have his eyes and lips. Both my sister Sheila and I have his physical features and his "smarts." Like him, I had an entrepreneurial spirit and started my psychotherapy practice. When mom caught me wringing my hands, she'd say, "your father used to do that." Both my father and I have Keratosis pilaris, a common skin condition with dry patches and tiny bumps on our elbows and knees. I met a few other relatives in Richmond with the same condition. I also inherited high blood pressure, which tragically was his silent killer, along with kidney disease. Fortunately, there is a lot more information known about high blood pressure and how it affects Black adults disproportionately than other races. Early diagnosis and treatment have helped me maintain my blood pressure.

Working on this project brought home a genuine appreciation of the sacrifices of the college-educated Blacks before me, who took advantage of the promises of educational opportunities available to third and fourth generations since the abolishment of slavery. As a psychotherapist, I have sat with many who grieved and healed from missing loved ones in their past. Now it's my turn to complete this journey of discovery and finally, be at peace with my identity and pedigree.

I believe it is my purpose to introduce the world to Clarence W. Newsome, Esq., another laborer for justice and equality during the Civil Rights Era. My goal is to ensure that my father's contributions to The Movement are entered into the Civil Rights Heroes Hall of Fame institutions throughout the country to solidify his legacy.

I hope that readers march in my father's shoes as I walk behind him, picking up strength, courage, and life-changing information along the way to continue to advance the path of freedom. I believe Millennials can pick up the torch in their own way. They can learn from the past and restructure the ongoing Movement to fit the current culture. My father was a man of commitment and determination. He chose to pursue a law career early in life, and in his college yearbook, he stated his intention to become a lawyer. He achieved his goal and accomplished many more before his untimely death at the age of 36. He made great strides as a Civil Rights attorney after only practicing for nine years. His selfless work is recorded in American history. Thank you, daddy Newsome, for leaving a fearless legacy of honor and service for your children, grandchildren, great-grandchildren, and generations to come. We know better, so we promise to do better.

With love and gratitude, Clarencia

THE DAILY NEWS

www.outspokenlawyer.com   The Blunt Truth   Since 1945

RICHMOND'S OUTSPOKEN LAWYER CHRONICLES

September 6, 1958

"I think the statement by the President showed a flagrant disregard for the actual facts staring him in the face, as well as for the supreme law of the land. By making such a statement he has made himself a pawn in the hand of the political overlord of the Southland. His statement has set back the tenor of integration 50 years. I cannot believe that the President is so poorly informed on such a vital domestic question or that he can so poorly judge the information before him."[3]

Attorney Clarence Newsome's response to President Eisenhower's "off-the-cuff" *remarks about a slower approach to desegregation in public schools.*

April 25, 1959

"Police used "Gestapo" tactics and as a result made some criminals out of innocent persons of the 164 arrested. Even if the beverages were being sold illegally at the city club, not all of the patrons knew it. The innocent men, women, and students have a record that they must carry through life. Negroes help to elect councilmen and this act of intimidation will not go unforgotten. The burden of proof is on the Commonwealth to prove that all persons arrested had knowledge of illegal activity."[4] *Attorney Newsome commented on the police raid of a Black club in Richmond, Market Inn, that had been in existence for 20 years without incident.*

February 22, 1960

"The protesting Negroes have a precedent to stand on."

"These laws very soon will be tested sooner than you think. Courts have held that a private company cannot discriminate against persons if it has invited those persons onto its premises."

Attorney Newsome referring to the VUU students arrested at Thalhimers Department store.

February 27, 1960

"The inability of African-Americans to use more than the basement of the library was humiliating, embarrassing, unfair, nauseating, and unconstitutional."

Attorney Newsome's statement after the arrest of Rev. Wyatt Walker and 10 others seeking to use the Petersburg, Virginia library main entrance and first floor. Protests led to the library closing for four months and ultimately became desegregated as a result of Newsome's petition.

March 19, 1960

"The practice of seclusion and segregation is unconstitutional. If the arrested party is convicted we will carry this case all the way to the Supreme Court, if necessary. And we will continue to fight this undemocratic city ordinance. Isn't the only reason the warrants were sworn out is because they were Negroes?"[5]

Attorney Clarence Newsome's remarks when three pastors

were arrested for praying in the library. Newsome received a telegram of congratulations and encouragement from the Rev. Martin Luther King Jr.

April 2, 1960

"Use the ballot box, the economic boycott, and then go in, sit down, and eat." *Attorney Clarence Newsome told a mass audience of approximately 600 people encouraging them to continue the store boycotts in Richmond.*[6]

March 1961

"Special emergency trespassing statutes enacted recently by the General Assembly aren't worth the paper they are written on from a legal point of view."

Attorney Clarence Newsome commenting to the press on the arrest for trespass of The Richmond 34.

May 12, 1962

"It's only fair play to elect a Negro council so that a minority group could be represented there."

"The lack of employment practices and promotion policies by our city government is of grave concern to the 90,000 Negro children of Richmond. Because of these unjust practices we come before our elected representatives to implore them to promote regardless of race, color, or creed."[7] *Attorney Newsome's remarks as part of his run for Richmond City Council advocating for equal pay for teachers and government workers.*

PART I

THE EARLY EARS

CHAPTER 1

YOUNG GIFTED AND BLACK

"The individual who can do something that the world wants done will, in the end, make his way regardless of his race."

- Booker T. Washington

My father, Clarence William Newsome, was born January 4, 1927, in Columbus, Ohio to Joseph Newsome and Clara Bell Hamm. That was the same year Calvin Coolidge became the 30th President of the United States of America, and the U.S. Supreme Court ruled in *Nixon v. Herndon* that the "white primary" law violated the Equal Protection Clause of the Fourteenth Amendment."[8] Although this important clause in the Constitution had been in place since 1868, Blacks were still viewed as inferior and bore the brunt of racism and brutality by whites.

The Newsome's did not come from wealth, but they had a strong work ethic and desire to succeed. My grandparents were working-class and they both instilled values and motivation to achieve greater than they could ever imagine. My dad and his three sisters, Evelyn, Naomi, and Claretta exceeded their parents' expectations.

His parents moved to Roanoke, Virginia when he was six years old. There were promises of better working opportunities in Virginia and when they settled, his father Joseph worked on the railroad and his mother Clara, worked as a maid at The Roanoke Hotel. This was the height of the Jim Crow Era in the south, so while his parents used their physical abilities to provide for their children, they planted the seed for their children to prioritize education and use their brains to become Black professionals.

All four children were subjected to segregation and graduated from the first all-Black Lucy Addison High School in Roanoke, Virginia, during 1941-1945. My father graduated from high school in 1945 and enrolled in the oldest of the original ten Historically Black Colleges, Virginia Union University (VUU), founded in 1865 right after the Civil War ended. Ironically, VUU is located on the land which was known to hold runaway slaves with help from the Freedmen's Bureau. During my father's college days, segregation's Jim Crow laws were in full effect and Black students could not matriculate into institutions of higher learning with white students.

I felt proud to learn that my father and his siblings were first generation college graduates. They were movers and shakers in their community and their generation of African-American college-educated youth. His sister, my aunt Naomi, went on to become the first Master's level Black Social Worker in Roanoke, Virginia. Indeed, they were trendsetters guided by my grandmother Clara, who held down the home when my grandfather Joseph had to pursue work in other cities. His youngest sister, Claretta graduated from Hampton University and pursued an administrative path and was trained as a computer key punch operator—like the human computer, Dorothy Vaughn, in the movie *Hidden Figures*. I was fortunate to speak to her once in my teens. She invited me to come to Virginia for the Jazz Festival as she and my father loved jazz. Little did she know that I lived a sheltered life in New Jersey and there was no way my mother was going to let me stay overnight in Virginia. I never spoke with my aunt Claretta again. She transitioned in July 2016 at the age of 76. Although there was an effort from cousins Kim and Joseph to find us, those efforts proved too late. I did send photos to Kim to share with other family members so they could have a visual of their New Jersey kin.

"Que'd" to Shine

VUU gave my father his first taste of leadership. Along with his studies, my dad was very active on campus. During his freshman year, he was Class Treasurer, President of the Pre-Law Club, and a member of the youth division of the NAACP. Later, he was elected as the State Youth Chairman for the support of President Harry Truman, a participant in the campus YMCA, and other Civil Rights organizations. If those roles weren't enough to keep him busy, he pledged Omega Psi Phi Fraternity. Last, but not least, he sang in the VUU Choir all four years and participated in the annual concert. Clarence Newsome left an indelible mark on VUU and graduated at 21-years old in 1949. He was honored by the Que's in the 1951-1952 Who's Who.

I guess the saying, "The apple doesn't fall far from the tree," is correct because I was very active in high school and joined many clubs. I also thrived in leadership in the Student Council, Yearbook Staff, Poetry Team, and I sang in the choir for all four years. I inherited my love for music and singing from both of my parents. *Daddy, you will never know how much I've longed to hear your voice.*

"When you feel really low
Yeah, there's a great truth you should know
When you're young, gifted and black
Your soul's intact..."
- Nina Simone

****

I believe human service is in our family DNA. People from childhood have shared with me that they could always turn to me for help and advice. They told me that I never judged them and often had a solution or helpful idea. I too was energized by things that were unfair, even in childhood. I often took up for the underdog and brought moral consciousness to the table. People teased me and said, "Here comes the voice of reason." I never knew these characteristics were reflections of my father until now.

I came across a note in my baby book where my mother made an entry which mentions that I was able to solve complex problems as a toddler. I could reason and strategize around obstacles in my way or problem solve obtaining what I wanted by constructing a method. Besides being articulate at an early age, she said that I was a bit aggressive with a temper. That sounds like my father whose superior linguistic skills and vocabulary astounded many. I have been called diplomatic because of my ability to mediate conflicts even during a heated therapy session between a couple or a mother and child. We are perceptive and know how to use the right words to hit the bullseye.

My mother always said my sister Sheila was smart like my dad. She attended college in Boston for two years and then transferred to VUU. Many professors and administrators remembered our father and spoke highly of him. Sheila had the ability to link thoughts together for critical analysis. She is great at parsing out the elements of an argument in a book, lecture or conversation in order to construct a counter-argument when needed. Sheila is a stickler for detail and inherited a quick wit, a sense of dignity, and a desire to fight for the downtrodden who are oppressed. Neither of us had any lawyer role models to imitate, so we chose the educational side of service. Sheila actually wanted to open her own school but changed her mind in hopes of teaching others to advocate for others in educational settings.

Sheila was called to the Christian ministry and studied Liberation Theology and theology from the perspectives of Black women at Boston University (BU). She integrated her interest in education, social justice and advocacy, in developing a program for renewal and education for black clergy in urban settings. She continues to be involved on the front line of social justice issues in the Black community. Currently in full-time ministry, she worked at BU's School of Theology for 20 years as an advocating Dean of Students for all students in the seminary.

I believe our father would be proud of how his daughters turned out.

My grandmother Clara Newsome.

My aunt Naomi Newsome, the first Master's level Black Social Worker in Roanoke, Virginia.

Aunt Claretta, a human computer like Dorothy Vaughn of NASA.

Clarence Newsome VUU Yearbook photo.

Clarence Newsome undergraduate degree from VUU, June 1949.

VIRGINIA UNION UNIVERSITY

ON THE RECOMMENDATION OF THE FACULTY
AND BY VIRTUE OF THE AUTHORITY VESTED IN THEM
THE TRUSTEES OF THE UNIVERSITY HAVE CONFERRED ON

CLARENCE WILLIAM NEWSOME

THE DEGREE OF
BACHELOR OF ARTS
THE DIVISION OF THE SOCIAL SCIENCES
AND HAVE GRANTED THIS DIPLOMA AS EVIDENCE THEREOF
GIVEN IN THE CITY OF RICHMOND IN THE STATE OF VIRGINIA
IN THE UNITED STATES OF AMERICA IN THE YEAR OF OUR LORD
ONE THOUSAND NINE HUNDRED AND FORTY-NINE
ON THE SEVENTH DAY OF JUNE

Theodore F. Adams
PRESIDENT OF THE BOARD OF TRUSTEES

J. M. Ellison
PRESIDENT OF THE UNIVERSITY

CHAPTER 2

HBCU STRONG

"Where you see wrong or inequality or injustice, speak out, because this is your country."

- Thurgood Marshall

After graduating from Virginia Union University, he enrolled at Howard University Law School in Washington, D.C., from 1950 - 1953 . It was during his pursuit of a law degree that he met my mother, Cora Florence Jeffries. My mom was in the graduate School of Social Work and was friends with his sister Naomi. I don't know the details of their love story, but love was obviously in the air, and they eloped in June, 1952. A few months later they had a wedding reception with my mother's family in New Jersey.

Social Engineers

"A lawyer's either a social engineer or he's a parasite on society."

- Charles Hamilton Houston

I believe my father's passion for justice and equality came from the tutelage of Dean Charles Hamilton Houston, known as the father of the "social experiment." Dr. Houston was the Dean of Howard University Law and the first legal counsel for the NAACP.[9] He chose to be a lawyer after serving in the military and witnessed the mistreatment of African-American soldiers. Dr. Houston stated, "*The hate and scorn showered on us Negro officers by our fellow Americans convinced me that there was no sense in my dying for a world ruled by them. I made up my mind that if I got through this war I would study law and use my time fighting for men who could not strike back.*"[10]

Dr. Houston coined the phrase that lawyers must be "social engineers" for change. Houston was committed to educating Howard's lawyers and preparing them to try NAACP cases. My father's law school class dedicated their yearbook to Houston.[11]Immediately upon my father's graduation in 1953, he was admitted to the Virginia Bar and practiced in Arlington, Virginia. Later that year, my older sister, Sheila was born premature. During those years there were no neonatal ICU's. Sheila was left for dead on a stretcher when a black nurse, who was also a missionary, found her and noticed that she was breathing. Sheila spent the first three months of her life in an incubator.

Following the advice and leadership of Dr. Houston, my father began working with the NAACP Legal Defense Fund and the Education Fund where he gained hands on oral argument experience and learned the art of legal brief writing with both black and white civil rights pioneers and legal scholars. A brief is a document filed with the court that states the facts and issues of your case and lays out your arguments using case law as to why you should win.

It's ironic that my mother and father eloped at Howard University. As fate would have it, I did the same thing. I had no idea about their elopement until *after* my mother's passing in 2017. She never mentioned it to me, but kept everything of sentimental value labeled in envelopes. While going through her papers one evening, I came upon an envelope labeled, "Papers Pertaining to Clarence." Inside the brown envelope was a receipt of her marriage and it listed the location as Washington, DC, June 1952.

While I attended Morgan State University, I eloped at 21 years old with Leon Shade Sr., during the summer of my junior year. I got married out of fear. I was not in love, but had sex a few times and feared becoming pregnant. Leon was five years my senior. He pressured me to marry him and in my guilt and naiveté, I agreed. I needed my birth certificate for the marriage so I came home to New Jersey while my parents were in California on a business meeting. I knew my mother would be devastated without a formal wedding, so I did not tell her until afterwards. She was not pleased initially, then daddy Duncan borrowed money to pay for the wedding.

As I was looking over the other documents in the "Clarence envelope," I recalled an early conversation with my mother when I was unable to carry a pregnancy to term. She told me about her miscarriage and how she started cramping. "When

Clarence got home, I was laying in a pool of blood!" I imagine she told me this story to reassure me that things happen to women that they often don't share, but that I had done nothing wrong. Since Sheila was born in 1953, it appears that my mom was pregnant when they eloped. It's not a big deal today, but back then, being a preacher's daughter would have been a stain on her character and the entire family.

After graduating from Morgan State, I got my first job as a social worker in the emergency room with Church Home Hospital, across the street from the highly regarded Johns Hopkins Hospital. At that time, I engaged in sporadic searches for information about my father. This was in 1977 when Alex Haley's *Roots* miniseries appeared on television. *Roots* touched the hearts of millions around the globe as Haley's story was based on his search for his African ancestral roots. Haley's efforts raised my consciousness about my father and my paternal family history.

I ordered The Yellow Pages from a few counties in Virginia. I began to search for my dad's family at my desk in the hospital emergency room. In between clients, I called the operator for people with the last name Newsome. The operator gave me three listings at a time. I called each one to find my Newsome relatives. Even though I rehearsed my telephone speech, my heart raced each time the phone rang as I had no idea who would be on the other end. Sometimes the answering machine came on so I hung up. After several calls, in September 1979, I somehow I reached the A.D. Price Funeral Home that buried my father.

Hello, this is Clarencia Newsome. I am the youngest daughter of Clarence Newsome. My father died when I was six years old. I'm calling because I'm in search of my Newsome relatives in Virginia. Are you related to Clarence Newsome?

This time there was a pause on the other end of the phone.

"Did you say you were Clarence Newsome's daughter?"

"Yes, I'm Clarencia Newsome."

"Your father was a good man," he said.

I felt the tears well up in my eyes which came easily because I was pregnant with my first child. My heart skipped a beat, I was trembling, and my palms grew sweaty. I swallowed hard as a gush of saliva welled up in my jaws. Not once have I ever heard those words. Mom mentioned on occasion that he was a brilliant lawyer. So when I first heard the news of his death at age six, I was unable to comprehend what it all meant. On this day it was different. There was a connection to my father that I never experienced before.

The funeral director knew the Newsome family well. He funeralized my aunt Naomi and grandmother Clara. He promised to send me programs of their services. The paging of a doctor on the PA system brought me back to focus. I had become comfortable speaking to this stranger about my family. Unfortunately, he did not have programs from my father's funeral but he dispelled the myth of my father's cremation and told me where my father was buried. Yet what he did next changed the trajectory of everything I had hoped for. I was eight and a half months pregnant and had so many questions about the Newsome family and mixed emotions.

"Is it OK if I call your cousin and give her your number?"
He asked.

"Of course! I would really appreciate it."

Within a few minutes, the phone rang at my desk and the woman on the other end introduced herself as my first cousin Kimberly. We talked as if we had known each other for years. Her warm and friendly tone along with her excitement immediately made me smile throughout the conversation. Her mother was my father's sister. I have one more first cousin, Joseph whom I have yet to meet. His mother is my father's youngest sister, Claretta who passed away in 2016.

After that initial conversation we both promised to keep in touch but did not do so for several years. I became very occupied with my newborn son and navigating through a rocky marriage. Kim and I picked up where we left off a few years later. We both filled in the blanks about our lives and now I had information about where my relatives were and I felt welcome visiting Virginia in the near future.

I lost touch with my cousin Kim for another few years when I left Baltimore. Now with my son Leon and my daughter, Sharm, I returned to New Jersey. I left home to pursue my degree and came back as a college-educated, single parent with two children. It didn't take long to skip payments on the furniture I had in storage, including a brand new kitchen set that I had been making payments on for nine months. I even had to get rid of a beautiful Steinway & Sons piano someone gave to me to improve my skills. Singing and playing the piano were a huge part of my life. Not having that piano was a huge emotional loss.

I had to take care of my children and grieve my marriage which left no energy or room to reach out to relatives. My primary focus was to find a job and get off welfare. I couldn't help but consider how eerily familiar my story was to my parents.' I kept thinking that history was repeating itself. After all, my parents eloped, they had two children who ended up in New Jersey with limited child support, and they were divorced. I was depressed, perhaps from post-partum, but also I never imagined my life taking this path at 29 years old. The mere thought of starting all over again was both frightening and embarrassing.

Thank God my parents received me back home with open arms. I lived with them for two years in Sheila's old bedroom and gave my old smaller room to my son. I was crushed and broken but the high expectations of my parents and with their support launched me forward. By grace, I was able to move out and relocate into a good neighborhood. Would you believe I lost cousin Kim's number and we did not speak for nearly 30 years!

Clarence W. Newsome and Cora F. Jeffries marriage license, June 1952.

No. 367769   **CERTIFICATE OF MARRIAGE**

I hereby certify that on this 27th day of June, 1952 at Washington, DC, Clarence William Newsome and Cora Florence Jeffries, were by me united in marriage, in accordance with the license issued by the Clerk of the United States District Court for the District of Columbia.

Name Rev. Augustus Lewis
Residence 2466 Ontario Rd NW

To be delivered to contracting parties.   16—14807-4 U. S. GOVERNMENT PRINTING OFFICE

My parents, shortly after their marriage, 1952.

My parents wedding reception in New Jersey.

Early family photo, mom, my father, babysitter, Sheila, and Santa.

CHAPTER 3

A CALL TO DUTY

*"The Negro race, like all races is going
to be saved by its exceptional men..."*
- **W.E.B. DuBois**

Harry S. Truman, the 33rd President of the United
States, fully desegregated the armed forces in 1948.
A few years later, my father served as a law clerk to
Belford V. Lawson, another Howard University alumni. Lawson was a civil rights attorney in the Washington, D.C. area
and made at least eight appearances before the U.S. Supreme
Court. He won *Henderson v. United States* in the 1950s with
the help of Thurgood Marshall.[12] The court in Henderson
held that segregation by race in train dining cars that traveled
across state lines was unconstitutional under the Interstate
Commerce Act.

During his clerkship with Lawson, my father was drafted
into the U.S. Army in May 1954. That same year, he was admitted to the Bar of the District of Columbia. As a college graduate,
he ranked as an officer. His unit was stationed in Berlin, Germany from May 1954 to February 1956. Always striving to do

more, he somehow found time to complete a degree program in Germany. He was granted a Certificate of Good Character and was honorably discharged. Upon his discharge, he received the Medal of Good Conduct.

After answering the call to serve his country, in January 1956, he returned to New Jersey where my mother was living in an apartment with her father. He was aware of the strides lawyers in the north were making to advance civil rights causes faster than in the south. My parents were part of the "the Great Migration" where Blacks were moving north in alarming numbers. It only made sense that he sought to practice law in New Jersey, so he studied for the New Jersey Bar. Like clockwork, I was born November 1956, less than 10 months following his return from Germany. Unfortunately, he was unsuccessful in passing the New Jersey Bar examination. I imagine the stress to provide for his family took a toll on his marriage. My parents separated shortly thereafter and my mom remained in New Jersey and my dad moved back to Virginia.

Returning to Virginia in 1956 was a pivotal time in my father's career. In 1956, Virginia adopted a Massive Resistance policy to block the desegregation of public schools that was mandated in the 1954 U.S. Supreme Court ruling of *Brown v. Board of Education.* To prevent desegregation, schools in several counties were shut down for nearly four years. The courts and law enforcement stepped in which added more racial tension to Virginia's caste system. Massive Resistance delayed large-scale desegregation of Virginia's public schools for years. [13]

My father worked on several school desegregation cases with other lawyers from the NAACP Legal Defense Fund including Ronald D. Ealy and Martin A. Martin. I found articles and images from the Afro-American newspaper on September 20, 1958 of my father along with Ealy and Martin leaving the Federal District Court in Richmond with three girls, Jane Cooper, Wanda Dabney, and Lorna Warden. The girls are seen smiling as they are leaving the federal hearing to admit them into a desegregated Richmond public school. At that time, there were 30 white and 24 colored schools in Richmond. The summer of 1958 was the first of many cases where colored children applied for admission to public schools and my father and his colleagues were on the front line of the majority of those cases.

The Talented Tenth

The Talented Tenth was attributed to an educated leadership class of African Americans in the early 20th century. Northern philanthropists first used the term, however it was publicized by W. E. B. Du Bois in an essay published in September 1903. This new ideology appeared in "The Negro Problem," a collection of essays written by leading African Americans including Du Bois, Paul Laurence Dunbar, and Booker T. Washington. The theory put forth a vigorous argument that the leaders of each race elevates the rest of the race. Thus, the argument not only makes the case against slavery but for the higher education of those capable of securing it due to their God-given intelligence. According to this theory, my father was indeed part of the Talented Tenth, as he was one of the best and brightest of his race with a college education. More importantly, his civil rights efforts would undoubtedly elevate the African American race to greatness from the top down. Oddly enough, although there were fewer women mentioned in DuBois' literature, my mother was a member of this elite group of learners as well. For this reason, my mother was a staunch advocate for higher education. My sister Sheila and I knew her expectations were high and the educational bar was raised for each of us year after year.

Shortly after the Talented Tenth principle, an emergence of the Black activism movement began. I believe that current racial inequality and segregation of my father's time influenced his decision to pursue a law degree. The National Association for the Advancement of Colored People (NAACP) had been in existence for eighteen years prior to his birth and he was determined to do his part to help the cause as soon as he graduated from law school. Years later, he ran for the local Richmond Chapter President of the NAACP and lost by only 70 votes.

Sketch of Clarence Newsome as an officer in the U.S. Army, Berlin, Germany 1955.

Me with my father at seven months old.

Early family photo: Me, Sheila, mom & my father.

CHAPTER 4

SILHOUETTE

*"All of us have moments in our childhood
where we come alive for the first time.
And we go back to those moments and think,
This is when I became myself."*

- Rita Dove

I
n August, 1957, my parents' phone number was selected
to win a 7-day trip to the Sir John Hotel in Miami, Florida. I found a detailed article in the Afro-American News
along with a photo of my parents, Sheila at 4 years old, and me
at 7 months old sucking two fingers. I was actually surprised
that our home address, 209 Avon Avenue in Newark, was published as well as the home address of my grandparents in Richmond. My mom's quote was the headline which read: "We'll be
forever indebted to both the hotel and the AFRO." She went
on to tell the reporter, "This is a most pleasant surprise and a
thrill for us. We plan to make this a combination vacation and
fifth wedding anniversary celebration.[14] The article mentioned
my father's educational and career background as well as my
mother's. It was interesting to see them in that celebratory light,

free from life's stresses. I wish I had a chance to ask my mother about that vacation.

Again, I think memories can play tricks on our mind. I'm amazed at how this one particular day after all these years, an interaction with my parents came to my mind as if it happened recently. I can actually recall a memory of my father when I was two years old. Unfortunately, it was not pleasant for my mother, but it was etched in my brain and recently surfaced. My father came for a visit to our apartment in Newark. I remember my mother being very excited and trying to finish my hairstyle. "Be still Clare, your father is coming!" Mom usually combed my hair in two braids and this time, only one side was complete. I had very thick kinky hair and my mother and grandmother's patience were much appreciated when they tried to bring it under control.

I'm not sure if he arrived early, but he appeared at the bottom of the steps. It seemed that before the visit there was a disagreement because there were no pleasantries exchanged. I was riding her hip and without hesitation, mom took the Fuller brush that she was using on my hair and threw it down the steps aiming for his head. She missed. I recall him saying, "You're a very foolish woman!" And just like that he was gone. To this day, that is the only memory I have of him.

My mother turned back to the room and walked to the mirror. She put me down and sat near the mirror and cried. I was stunned and confused. I had only seen her cry once before. I looked in the mirror with both hands under my chin and said, "are you going to finish my hair?" She replied, "It doesn't matter now. He's gone anyway."

"Will he be back?"

"No," she answered and turned away from me.

I was concerned about my mother crying so I believe that memory was hidden from me and totally out of my consciousness for many years. Actually, that's the way it's been lately, on again and off again memories.

I pressed her and asked, "When would my daddy be back?" She blurted, "that was your daddy!" Her response did not match the initial enthusiasm she had prior to his arrival. I imagine she was expecting a better reunion. She later mumbled, "Maybe he will come back home." Apparently, that never happened and he relocated to Richmond for good.

In talking with Sheila, she remembers our father as more of a shadow. She has the same memory of them having a disagreement on the steps of our second floor apartment in Newark. She remembers him standing on the first floor at the bottom of the entry steps that lead to the second floor where mom was standing holding me. Sheila said that I was crying and she was also crying because the tension and words were strong. She recalls our father looking at her smiling. She thought to herself, *he's real, he's not a ghost.* She was at the top of the steps. Sheila wanted to run downstairs to that smile, but she felt locked in place, and then he turned and walked out the door. She will never forget his eyes, his mustache, and his smile. He left an empty space that she holds onto—keeping him frozen at the bottom of the steps, even now.

My parents divorced in October 1959. His law firm colleague, Martin A. Martin, handled the divorce. Once my father left New Jersey and returned to Virginia, his career began to blossom, but the pay for Black lawyers was little to nothing. Yet my mother needed child support and the formal paperwork was filed and sent via U.S. mail between Richmond and East Orange. Years later, I read the personal correspondence between them and it seemed polite, but very formal.

In one typed letter, he advised my mother that he would be sending the child support as it becomes due. He also mentioned in the letter, "Give my regards to Sheila and Clarencia." Reading those words made my heart tilt to the side as I mused, *his regards?* Whatever that meant it felt special. I was most impressed by his signature. His handwriting was graphic and neat. His signature was broken in half as if it were two words: "New Some." I can see why he was often the secretary in organizations if not the chairman. Later in his career he was the corresponding secretary for the NAACP Redress Committee as well as the secretary of the Richmond Crusade for Voters, and Chairman of the Committee Against Juvenile Delinquency.

In September of 1960, I began kindergarten in elementary school. My mother walked me to school and I was proud to be in a learning environment. While I was learning basic skills, my father was winning cases in U.S. courtrooms over 300 miles away. At the time, The Richmond 34 case was on the news. My father was the lead attorney for that case and I remember my mom shouting, "He's going to get himself killed," as she stared at the news on TV.

That fear of losing our black men to premature, violent deaths at the hands of police and for speaking out against discrimination, is just as strong today as it was back then. The rise in police incidents of brutality in Black neighborhoods. Whether it's driving while black, breathing while black, eating while black, or even walking into your own house while Black, has caused injury or even death to Black people. We are witnessing overt actions of Nationalist rhetoric and hate groups who are determined to turn the clock backwards and heighten violence, prejudice, and inequality across America. I was shocked to see that other countries were listing travel advisories for people of color because traveling to the United States could be risky if you were a Black man.

The roll call of deaths of the names of young and middle-aged Black men targeted and profiled by the police is alarming. Just like there were good guys and bad guys of different races in law enforcement, Black police trust has diminished. Ironically, my mother's concerns for my father's welfare was based on facts not feelings. To describe it better, it's what every Black person felt when President Barack OBama was elected. The fear may have been unspoken, but everyone held their breath because no one wanted to see him or his family hurt or killed. There were internet prayer chains of Black people praying for Obama all eight years in office.

As the mother of a son, the same fear came close to home many times. I was hypervigilant about my son's car being in good working order in hope to lessen his chances of being pulled over. When he had outstanding tickets, I paid them until he matured and became more responsible. This type of fear can be debilitating. I remember one year when my son was home from Rutgers and we went to buy a Christmas tree. Somehow, my son and a middle-aged white man got into an argument. I found all five foot two inches of me standing in-between two grown men because I feared the worse. Thankfully calmer heads prevailed and Christmas was a joyous family celebration.

Letter to my mother from my father's attorney, Martin A. Martin,
regarding the initial divorce filing.

Law Offices
Hill, Martin & Olphin
118 East Leigh Street
Richmond 19, Virginia

Oliver W. Hill
Martin A. Martin
James R. Olphin

8   April   1959

M.Plan 8-9033
8-9034

Mrs. Cora J. Newsome,
310 Seymour Avenue,
Newark, New Jersey.

Dear Mrs. Newsome:

As attorney for your husband, Clarence W. Newsome, on yesterday I filed a bill for divorce against you on the ground of desertion. In all probability, the papers will be served upon you in person within the next few days. However, I thought it advisable to explain these matters to you in advance so that you would not be unduly worried about this matter, particularly since I understand that you have two infant children born of this marriage.

I further understand that Mr. Newsome is now paying to you through the Juvenile and Domestic Relations Court of the City of Richmond, Virginia, support money for these children. Mr. Newsome tells me that he has no wish or desire to change the matter of custody of the children or the support money for the children at the present time and will continue to pay this support money as it becomes due.

I would also like to let you know that a divorce on the ground of desertion is one of the legal grounds for a divorce in Virginia, and casts no moral reflection upon either party. Certainly in this suit there is nothing which can reflect upon your character or reputation and I do not believe that you will be damaged financially by loss of support money.

This letter is just to explain these matters to you so that you would not be unduly alarmed when you receive the papers.

If there is any further information which I can give you relative to this matter, please advise me.

Very truly yours,

Martin A. Martin

MAM:rbs

Letter to my mom from my father sending his regards to Sheila and me.

Law Offices
Hill, Martin & Olphin
118 East Leigh Street
Richmond 19, Virginia

Oliver W. Hill
Martin A. Martin
James R. Olphin

Milton 8-9073
8-9074

7   October   1959

Mrs. Cora Newsome,
310 Seymour Avenue,
Newark, New Jersey.

Dear Mrs. Newsome:

It has occurred to me that upon receipt of this decree and check you may want to consult with your attorney. This thought occurs in view of the letter of September 23, 1959, from your court. It is not sufficient to say which is paramount, the decree as entered or the letter from the New Jersey Domestic Relations Court - particularly as it applies to visitation rights, etc. Now, the court has given me until January 1, 1960, to take care of the small arrearage in view of the order entered in the decree.

However, please find my check enclosed pursuant to the order of the decree.

I hope that we shall be able to adjust our differences in regard to the above amicably. My regards to Sheila and Clarencia.

Sincerely   yours,

Newsome

Encls. - 2

The last page of the final divorce document from my father's attorney indicating that my father was currently paying child support.

7. That your complainant is now, and has been for more than one year next immediately preceding the commencement of this suit, an actual bona fide resident of and domiciled in the City of Richmond, in the State of Virginia.

8. That there were two children born of this marriage, namely, Sheila Diane Newsome, age 5; and Clarencia Rene Newsome, age 2, both of whom are now in the custody of the defendant, but are being supported by complainant, and complainant at this time does not request any change in said custody or support.

WHEREFORE, complainant prays that he be awarded a divorce from the bond of matrimony from the defendant on the ground of desertion.

CLARENCE W. NEWSOME, Complainant,

By _____
Of Counsel.

MARTIN A. MARTIN, ESQ.,
113 East Leigh Street,
Richmond 19, Virginia.

Attorney for Complainant.

My parents' divorce abstract.

V.S. Form 50
10-56—30M

ABSTRACT OF DIVORCE DECREE
COMMONWEALTH OF VIRGINIA
DEPARTMENT OF HEALTH—BUREAU OF VITAL STATISTICS

STATE FILE NO. 4265

Place (city or county) ___Richmond___ Date of decree ___8/26/59___

Plaintiff ___Clarence W. Newsome___ Age ___ Color ___Negro___

Residence _____ Birthplace ___unkn___

Occupation* _____ Industry or business _____

Defendant ___Cora Jefferies Newsome___ Age ___ Color ___Negro___

Residence _____ Birthplace ___unkn___

Occupation* _____ Industry or business _____

Date of marriage ___6/27/52___ Place ___Washington, D. C.___

Duration of marriage _____ Number of minor children affected ___two___

Cause of divorce ___wilful desertion___

Divorce granted to: Husband ☒ Yes ☐
Wife ☐ Was case contested: No ☒ Alimony granted: No ☒ Yes ☐

Kind of divorce ___Bond of matrimony___ Signature ___Richard McDonald___

Date of separation ___4/1/58___ Deputy Clerk of ___Hustings Ct., Part II___

Send only Bed and Bd.-Absolute-Annulment
* If wife has no gainful occupation say housewife

All above information
as at time of decree

CHAPTER 5

MY TWO DADS

*"When we lose one blessing, another is often
most unexpectedly given in its place."*
- **C.S. Lewis**

I was too young to remember when my parents got divorced. Yet I recall my stepdad, Alfonso Duncan being around early in my life. My mom, my sister Sheila and me, moved into my uncle's house on Shepard Avenue in East Orange, New Jersey. Mr. Duncan lived next door on the second floor with his mother. Mom and Mr. Duncan spent lots of time together after work and he took us on outings around New Jersey. We often went to the park and he never seemed to get tired pushing Sheila and me on the swings.

I recall the night my sister and I were in bed giggling and peeking at mom and Mr. Duncan on a date. That night was special because Mr. Duncan proposed to my mom in the living room. He was down on one knee, and we heard her say "Yes!" The wedding was held at Messiah Baptist Church on Oak Street, less than three blocks from our house on Shepard Ave. In June, 1960, when I was only four years old, I was the flower girl in my mom and Mr. Duncan's wedding. It was an exciting day.

I didn't think it was odd to be getting a "new daddy" because I did not recall a bond with my father. However, I formed a bond with Mr. Duncan instantly. He was fun, strong, and very loving. I remember attending the wedding rehearsal the night before. I knew what to do and I made sure to smile and walk to the beat of the organ music. Everyone told me how well I performed my job. Sheila and I sat with Grandma Duncan. Daddy Duncan looked handsome in a dark suit and white shirt and my mother had on a cream dress and a hand full of red, pink, and white flowers. I felt so special to be a part of the wedding. It was a proud day for me and my sister.

My mom, and new dad were off to Niagara Falls for their honeymoon. My maternal grandmother Nana, was on duty to take care of Sheila and me. I remember my heart leaped when the phone rang. The large black phone on the coffee table startled me. It had such a loud, dull ring. I picked up the heavy receiver and heard my mom and new daddy's voice. My sister also spoke to them. They promised to bring me something sweet. When they returned, they gave me the biggest rainbow swirl lollipop I had ever seen! Sheila got one too.

Daddy Duncan was handsome and muscular. He was a baseball player and looked sharp in his white and blue baseball uniform. He loved all sports, except hockey. His favorite team was the Brooklyn Dodgers, "Boys of Summer." He also cheered for the underdog, New York Mets. Daddy's number one football team was the Green Bay Packers, led by one of the greatest sports leaders of all time, Vince Lombardi.

Daddy Duncan worked at General Motors (GM) and took us to see how cars were made on the assembly line in Linden, New Jersey. He worked on the line until he was promoted to a Paint Store Manager. He loved everything about cars: inspecting them, naming them, and of course driving them. He had this sense of pride in his voice when he described to Sheila and me how cars worked. Sheila says that she still hears his driving voice commands, "Lean into the curve. Do not pass a truck in the curve. Keep your speed even. Use your signals. Check your oil. Warm up the car."

Daddy was a gentleman and made every effort to help women. He never allowed my mom or us to lift or carry anything. It was his job to lead and take care of his household of women. He shoveled, he raked, he saw to every detail about his family.

He was present for every school event for both Sheila and me. He checked all report cards and encouraged us to do our best. He hovered with care in order to protect. He loved deeply. At times, underneath all that caring felt a bit smothering. He checked everything two times or more for safety. Every sentence or lesson came with a gesture or exclamation to emphasize a point. Sheila and her husband can imitate his gestures and speeches. She even taught her daughter his phrases and gestures so she could learn what her stroke-impaired "Poppa" expected from his girls.

From what I've read, I believe my father was raised Baptist. Daddy Duncan was a Bible reader and faithful church attender. He was a deacon and treasurer for the church for decades. He was the yin to my mother's yang. Working for the church the strength of their relationship was most visible. Daddy Duncan read the newspaper every day and bought three on Sunday. He bought Sheila the New York Times without fail. Sheila loved to read and she devoured the Sunday Times after church. One Sunday she round found a recruitment ad for a graduate program in Education in Vermont. Before we knew it, daddy was packing Sheila's belongings in a U-Haul and she was headed to Vermont to obtain a master's degree.

Although daddy was not a legal scholar like my father, he was very intelligent. I'd consider him a "race man." He was always talking about discrimination against the Black man. He had many examples from his job at GM and his daily interactions. I can still hear him say, "The white man will keep his foot on the neck of the Black man!" I believe that his thoughts and conversations about race and discrimination would have been similar to my father's views. Words are not adequate to describe the love and appreciation I have for daddy Duncan. He demonstrated unconditional love for his "three girls," and provided for us in every way possible for over 50 years. Mom, Sheila, and I experienced Black love at its finest!

Sheila (age 7) and me (age 4) after my mom's wedding to Alfonso Duncan at Grandma Duncan's house.

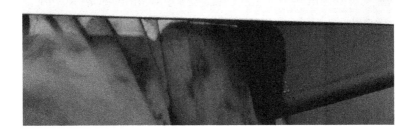

CHAPTER 6

BLENDED FAMILY

---

*"You don't choose your family. They are
God's gift to you as you are to them."*

- Bishop Desmond Tutu

D espite the sheltering, I was not exempt from the trauma and fallout of being a stepchild. My loving stepfather's family was not pleased that he was marrying a divorced woman with two children. In particular, my stepfather's cousin Iris, despised my mother and would almost snarl when she looked at us. On Christmas, the gift-giving also displayed partiality when my cousins were inundated with lavish gifts and my sister and I received one gift each of mediocre value. I was a second-class Duncan and often reminded that there was not one drop of Duncan blood in me. The pain felt like a double rejection and my identity was complicated by the lack of kindness that adults were supposed to demonstrate to a small child.

I was surrounded by my mom's family, and my maternal grandmother, Effie whom we referred to as Nana, Aunt Cassie (Nana's only sister who lived next door) and her husband, my

Uncle James. My stepdad was one of four boys and his younger brother's sons became known to me as my cousins. When we were around my daddy Duncan's mother, it was like being with royalty. She was a kind, classy woman and a member of the Eastern Star. In her home, she showcased beautiful glasses, dishes, and silverware that she purchased from Hayne and Company where she was a maiden in the bathroom. Her job was to make sure women had everything they needed to feel comfortable. I recall when Sheila and I visited her on the job. She wore a fancy gray uniform with white lace and a matching cap and apron. She was very proud to see us when my daddy took us to the Newark store. Grandma's white supervisor greeted us with pleasantries, yet she scooted us along to make sure we did not extend our visit and distract Grandma from her duties.

It's funny how memories like going to Grandma Duncan's job from so long ago are still fresh in my mind. I imagine it's because it was a significant moment in my life. I also remember when I was around five years old and my father called to speak to my sister and me. We were a complete family in the Duncan household so I didn't comprehend who was on the other line, but I was eager to have a turn to speak to him since no one ever called to speak to Sheila and me. However, my sister's brief conversation ended abruptly when she began to cry. I'll never know what he said to her and I could not make out the sound of his voice. My mother grabbed the phone and shouted, "If you are going to upset her, don't call!" She slammed the phone down and hung up on him. *Wait. What about my turn to speak?* I thought. I recall feeling angry at my mother and the person on the other end of the line whom she called my father, because I did not have a turn. Nana escorted Sheila and me to our bedroom, while my mother sat on the couch breathing heavily with her eyes closed.

As a child, I bounced back from that episode quickly. A few times I recall my grandmother making comments to my mother about my "real" father. Somehow it did not matter because I was unsure of what a "real" father meant. All I knew was that there was Alfonso Duncan and I was his shadow. Everywhere he went, I wanted to go. I bonded with him and had no physical or emotional connection with the man on the phone living in Richmond, Virginia or any other man for that matter. Although I sensed he was important to Sheila and me because mom and grandma were excitable when they mentioned him, I numbed him out of my mind and emotions because I had no choice! I was just too young to understand my father's role and his importance in my life until it was too late.

The Name Game

"The most beautiful sound I ever heard:
Maria, Maria, Maria, Maria
All the beautiful sounds of the words
In a single word:
Maria, Maria, Maria, Maria…"
- **Larry Kent, Westside Story**

As a youngster, everyone called me Clare. I was very alert and outspoken like my father at home. One day I started asking my mom questions. "What's my real name?" "How do you spell it?" "I'm named after who?" I told my mother that I thought my name was beautiful. She believed it was too cumbersome for me to spell, but I convinced her that I could do it. I begged her to make it official at school. She did so without complaint, even though everyone during my school years called me Clare, without the "i." I now had two names and two dads. *Clarencia, Clarencia, Clarencia the most beautiful name I ever heard.* I loved my name. I felt like the beautiful "Maria" the young man sang about in *West Side Story*.

In 1964 I used Clare on all of my schoolwork. Then in 1965, I was registered as Clarencia Newsome. I lived the dual loyalty and legacy for the rest of my life. Deep down, I was happy to have my father's name in the Duncan household. Whenever my mother talked about my father I had butterflies inside and I would light up even though the stories were few and far between. Once, she told me, "You're named after him you know. We thought you were a boy." My mother had premature and stillborn children before and after me. I was the only child she carried full term. She went on to tell me how the Germans pronounced his name when he was in the military: the last "ce" sound is a hard "ch." In the Army he was referred to as "Clarench." When I heard that name it made me giggle as it reminded me of a Dr. Seuss character.

In the south, when African-American families expected a boy and it turned out to be a girl, they had creative ways of showing a daughter's lineage. They simply adjusted the girls' name to coincide with her father's name. So, William became Wilhelmina, Thomas became Thomasina, Frederick became Fredricka, and in my case Clarence became Clarencia. Many cultures have naming ceremonies because your name is believed to shape your identity. In the Jewish culture, the father will name his firstborn son after his grandfather. Even in the Bible we see the importance of lineage and who begat who for centuries. Additionally, in West African culture, you are given two names at birth. One name is the day you were born, and the other name is a characteristic your family hopes will become your life's pattern or path.

Still, as a young person, there were times of confusion as to my identity. In school I would sign my last name as Duncan and other times Newsome. Concerned teachers called my mother in for a conference after they found out that my sister Sheila was doing the same thing. I vaguely remember a conversation daddy Duncan had with us about why he wasn't adopting us. He assured us that it was not because he loved us any less. He merely felt that one day it would be important to have my father's last name out of respect. *Thank you daddy Duncan, you were so right!* Things have a way of working out for the best because if daddy Duncan had adopted Sheila and me, we would not have been eligible to receive our father's social security benefits after his death in 1963. Those early government funds helped meet our household expenses and allowed both of us to go to college. The benefits continued until we were 22 years old.

In reality, how do we know if the names handed down by our grandparents and parents are accurate? There are millions of names that will never be known due to slavery, lynchings, and other killings of innocent Black people. Our last names are how we determine our ancestral lineage. Yet it's the first names that our parents give us that is supposed to determine our destiny. The name "Clarence" means bright, shining and gentle in Latin. It is also associated with British royalty in the 19th Century. The name "Sheila" means heavenly or of the heavens. History demonstrates that my father was bright, passionate, and a shining light for African Americans. My sister Sheila and I achieved academic and career success, so I believe we both have made our "three" parents proud.

The American Dream

I was earshot when my mom and daddy Duncan were in a heated argument. They never argued so this memory stands out. They were having a new house built from the ground which was very rare during that time. We were all involved in the process from the blueprints to the foundation. I remember the sweet smell of the wood framing when we visited to check on the progress.

Once we moved in, everything was going smoothly until this one argument. Tensions flared when I heard daddy Duncan say, "This is not my house. This is Clarence Newsome's house!" I was frozen in my tracks. *What did he mean? There was that name again.* By this time I was able to ask my mother what he meant by this statement and why was he so angry. Up to that point, I did not know that he even got angry with her.

My mother later explained that she had been saving my father's social security payments sent on our behalf in a special account. When the time came for building the house, she used those funds to make the down payment. At once I felt that odd but familiar conflict of pride versus shame. I was happy that because of my father we had a beautiful home, but upset that our comfortable new home made my stepdad angry and uncomfortable.

I think that episode began the love triangle between my mother and my two dads. That conversation with my mother increased my pride and my pain at the same time regarding Alfonso Duncan and Clarence Newsome. It was hard to love one and not the other. I was sad that Clarence died so young at 36 in the height of his career. I also had to bypass the negative narrative of my grandmother who often spoke of my father in less than glowing terms. My grandmother was a sanctified woman and had no tolerance for anyone who was "still in the world" partying and drinking. She could not understand that my father was a socialite and a large part of the events he attended was to bring attention to and connect those with financial means to help fight for his firms civil rights cases.

I was very opinionated and had to be corrected often about interrupting adult conversations with my thoughts. I introduced myself to others at age four as "ouchy," a nickname I inherited from the agony of my mother and my Nana combing through my thick black hair. Sometimes the family laughed at my verbal wit. Other times my mouth earned me a punishment.

Little did I know that my assertiveness, effective communication skills, and perseverance were traits passed down from my father. I always had compassion for others and was never afraid to back down from an argument. In hindsight, I believe that I would have been a great litigator, but at six years old, my *real* father was gone, and I had no legal role models nor an understanding of his life's work.

CHAPTER 7

ACTIN OUT

"From the moral as from the intellectual
point of view, the child is born neither
good nor bad but master of his destiny."
- **Jean Piaget**

I started to display signs of antisocial behavior in my pre-teens. I experienced symptoms of depression, but it never showed up at school or church. I was a hero kid, a term used to describe children who come from dysfunctional families. I distracted the world with my grades, and performance in the band, on stage, or directing the youth choir. But when my other negative feelings showed up, I buried them instead of sorting them out.

I was funny, witty, and often the comic relief for my family. When I was happy, I was happy, but when I was walking on the dark side of the moon I didn't know how to act. I was a girl of paradoxes. Current psychological research now includes dysfunctional behaviors to unresolved grief. At home I would go into fits of rage and compulsive overeating. By sixth grade, I was grossly overweight for a child my age and height. I learned to ease my pain with food until my stomach was so full that my inner emotions were smothered. I lived in two realities: the outside bubbly Clare or the dark out of control Clare.

In our home there was never a need that I had that went unmet. Except for one thing— knowing more about Clarence Newsome. There was a huge void that I needed filled to help me feel better about myself and good about my father. I was filled with rage and would fight both boys and girls in the school yard. I had begun shoplifting from corner stores and stealing change out of my daddy's valet. I even managed to sneak a bottle of Andre Brut Champagne into the house and drank the entire bottle, without a care that my parents were in the next room. I lied whenever it was convenient.

To the outside world, I was a model honor roll student. The dual life manifested in many ways. I would have angry fits in my room and destroy my own things. One night I tore my favorite housecoat in several places only to be remorseful later and repaired it with the sewing kit my mom kept in the hallway closet. I hated my body, but thought I had a pretty face. My sister Sheila was petite and a size three or five. I was a chubby and struggled with my weight.

In desperation, my mother took me to the doctor who prescribed diet pills which at that time contained speed. Once I bought into the idea of controlling my weight with pills, I began yo-yo dieting and starved myself all day to lose weight. I was a size 14, but I was "thick" as the young people phrase it today. Although I was not diagnosed schizophrenic, I had two personalities. The pills made my moods and personality that more exaggerated from one extreme to the other. With my friends, I was humorous and a daredevil. But to my teachers, parents, and church leaders I was very subdued.

My two greatest joys were music and baton twirling. I temporarily taught younger children the piano during the summer to make extra money. I was given a decent allowance of $1.00 each week and loved visiting The Bandwagon Corner Record Store every Friday to get the newest music single for .79 cents. I actually enjoyed sad music like "Love On A Two-Way Street" and "Lonely Girl." I was also quite a dancer and would jam to "Jimmy Mack" and "Dancing in the Street." I even listened to music from the 50s like Sam Cooke and the Platters, but my teenage years were a bumpy ride. I didn't really know who I was, but I knew who I was *supposed* to be.

I grew up in an era where you were known by your last name. If you were a Johnson, you carried yourself in a way that was respectable to your family name. Being a Duncan came with white gloves and crinoline dresses with wide sashes around the waist. We were a church going family which imposed another set of rules and standards. The community was the watchdog and everybody told on you if you were out of line. I know this type of atmosphere saved many lives. It was easier to be on the straight and narrow, but it came with a lot of pressure. My mother was a highly successful executive with a Masters Degree in Social Work. She outpaced several whites in her career and worked for Newark's Children's Aid Society. We were well groomed and taught etiquette. Sheila and I curtsied, and we never had to be reminded to say "please" and "thank you."

No one would have ever expected me to be hiding another self below the surface.

Sheila and I were not subjected to corporal punishment per se. She was more often verbally rebuked for things, and they were few and far between. She held her anger and her tongue. Instead of reacting, she would retreat to her room and read tons of books. She was much more passive than me, but Sheila suffered from headaches and stomach aches. I got my only real whipping when I refused to stop taking shortcuts through the neighborhood backyards with my friend Jeffrey. I had been warned several times. The last time I got caught, I was prepared for my fate.

When my mother got home from work, I was lying across my bed with the black leather belt placed strategically near me. I waited for her and confessed. Yes, she went to town on me that day! Again, that was rare. Punishment for me was usually pop in the mouth for injecting into adult conversation or being rude to an adult. I remember going to church to apologize to one of the senior mothers after I told her, "I don't have to listen to you, you are not my mother!" My mother stood by giving me a stern look.

My Nana also punished me with no TV when I felt the urge to talk back to her. She was our babysitter while mom worked. I took food and snacks from the pantry without permission every chance I got. One day my grandmother caught me and an argument ensued. I went toe-to-toe with my grandma. I said something mean to her and it was the only time I heard my saintly missionary grandmother curse. She told me she would whip my butt. She did not whip me, but I had to apologize. My punishment was that I could not listen to my favorite radio show with Cousin Brucie. No Beach Boys. No Supremes for an entire night.

I displayed the symptoms of a traumatized child with unresolved grief. However, I can't blame it all on my father's death as there were other unnerving events that happened during my preteens. There were sexual predators exposing themselves in the neighborhood, and the kidnapping and death of a friend whom I witnessed getting into an unfamiliar car, never to return. The same boys asked me to get into the car also but I said no and followed my parents' rules of not getting into cars with strangers. My friend was found dead in a catholic church basement. After that incident, I was so traumatized that I refused to get into the car with my uncle!

CHAPTER 8

CLOSE CONNECTIONS

"Healthy children will not fear life if their elders
have integrity enough not to fear death."
- Erik Erikson

By the time I became a teenager, I was perpetually sad about my father's early death in a way that was apparent to my mother. When it came to Clarence Newsome, I was sad that I had no memory of him and that he would never know me. I remember crying inconsolably on my sixteenth birthday because I didn't know if I looked like him. I felt the pressure to be responsible, smart, and to represent the brilliant mind I was told he had. I missed my father without memories and I sensed that I was being disloyal to my daddy Duncan for being sad. This was quite a lot to handle for a growing teenager. I did not always handle these feelings well. I was an emotional wreck at times. I was still shoplifting, feeling justified that what had been taken from me, gave me the right to take whatever I wanted. My mother couldn't figure out why I was so angry during my fits of rage. One day in an outburst I screamed, "because I will never know him! I don't know what he looks like and I don't know if he loved me!"

My mom kept a treasure trove of photographs from her college years at Howard University. She reassured me that my father loved me. This is when I was introduced to "the blue suitcase." It had her initials engraved at the top, "CFJ" (Cora Florence Jeffries). She brought it upstairs to my room and gave me free access to her scrapbook memories of cousins and other family members and pictures of my father. This was her way of allowing me to be close to my father.

From that day forward, she agreed that I could keep the suitcase under my bed. Whenever the urge hit my soul, I climbed out of bed, sat on the floor and pulled out the blue suitcase. Each time I opened it, the smell of old film from the past flooded my senses. It was almost like transporting me through time. There were multiple family photos and a few pictures of my father. He was so handsome and I definitely have his eyes and eyebrows. Looking at photos of my father washed away 16 years of pain and uncertainty. For the first time, we were reunited at least on some level and it felt really good.

Not long after I received the blue suitcase, I spoke with my grandma Clara and my aunt Claretta. I asked my mother for my paternal grandmother's phone number. She readily agreed and supplied the number. I remember sitting on the side of the bed in Sheila's room and lifting the handset to dial grandma Clara's number on Sheila's yellow princess phone.

"Hello."

Hearing grandma Clara's voice for the first time was surreal. It was as if time stood still. I had a voice on the other end of the phone who knew my father.

"Hi grandma Clara. This is Clarencia. I've wanted to speak with you for a long time and my mom says it's OK."

Our conversation was brief and she asked about school and my sister. She agreed to write to me. I received two letters from her and then for some reason, all contact was broken. I can still see the pink stationery and matching envelope I had purchased to write her my first letter. A few days later I received a call from my Aunt Claretta, my father's youngest sister.

"Hello Clarencia. This is Aunt Claretta."

"Hello."

"It's so good to hear your voice. My mother told me that you want to hear as much about your father that we remember."

"Yeah that would be great because I really only have a few pictures."

"Well, you know that I am the youngest but the thing I remember most about him was his car. He always drove a convertible. He used to take me for rides with the top down and everyone stared at us."

"Really? Do you have any pictures of him in the car?"

"I'm not sure but I can check with a few other family members."

"OK."

"Another thing I remember is that he was the only person I had ever seen with a round bed. It was beautiful and weird at the same time."

I remember giggling when she said that.

"Wow. I have never seen a round bed before."

"Yes, it was different. He liked really nice things and was such a sharp dresser. Everything had to be crisp."

Aunt Claretta invited me to come to Virginia at any time. I asked my mom why nobody from that side of the family ever looked for me and my sister. I don't recall her answer but I was satisfied for the time being that I could find them if needed. I never made it to Virginia during those early years, nor did I speak to my aunt Claretta again.

In my head, the fantasies about my father would ebb and flow. One time my curiosity was met with a prickly rebuke from my mother who shouted, "Stop messing in it! Clare, I won't keep letting you pull me back there!" At the time, I couldn't understand how she equated questions about my father as a dig or reference to her. After that, she announced a moratorium and told me that once I was fully grown, that I could do whatever I wanted, but she was done with being grilled by me. I learned how to become more loyal to my new family by not bringing Clarence's name up again until much later. There was always a bit of detachment that I learned to live with and certain emotions I masked to appease her.

Letter from my grandmother Clara when I was 16 years old.

7 – 15 – 69

my dear Granddaughter
I recieved your loving
letter it found me very well
glad to no you all are ok...
yes Clara I waited for answer
from you all but I knew you
all had to get your lesson and
did not have time but thats
is alright as long as you
dent for get me, for I never
will for you all, give your
mother and shelia my love

Well Clara you are going to Camp
That is nice. I Will write you if
I have thing have got one of
your cousin from new york
Keeping him this summer he is
only 5 year old, he is my fady
girl little boy. Clara as soon
as I can have some pitcure
made off the one of your daday I
Will send you and shelia
one, so you all keep sweet
for I love both of you all
answer when you have time
over

and I will write you a gain
real soon. I wish your
mother would let yer all
come down to see me this
summer, I have another grand
daughter in New york she is
15 years old she will be to see
me next month, so be sweet
girl with love your
grandmother
Clara Newsome

My dad visiting his sister, my aunt Claretta in
New York, late 1950s.

CHAPTER 9

CHILDREN OF THE MOVEMENT

"My hope for my children is that
they respond to the still, small
voice of God in their own hearts.

- *Andrew Young*

Early in my studies as a psychotherapist, I learned that one of the biggest tasks for adolescence is identity. I experienced my identity crisis in my teens and my "daddy issues" had not been dealt with until my late adult years. According to Erik Erickson, the period of adolescence is the beginning of challenging the identity your parents gave you with the identity you feel inside. It can be a stormy and problematic time for teens and family members. More than likely teens experience different moods every hour or every day and without everyone scrambling for cover. Since the hormones are quickly changing as well as psychological and emotional changes, this can be a period of dangerous alcohol and drug experimentation as well as social experiences on the edge. For those teens struggling with identity and acceptance into a peer group find their unfinished business with a deceased or absent parent as fuel for their internal fire.

Young children struggle to understand the concept of death. By adolescence they may have a greater understanding, but may be focused on what they feel they have lost.[15] Experts say that children need to hear the word "dead" and to hear it in a quiet gentle way that their parent is not coming back.[16] Children are always listening, and adults must be cognizant of their reactions and the way they handle death and other bad news to not traumatize the child. I have read many scholarly articles on delayed grief in adults and children. Even if the loss was not a traumatic sudden loss, the child experiencing the loss may experience trauma.

Within the culture of African American households, children were expected to be seen but not heard. This meant that as a child you absolutely had to stay out of grown folks' business or an adult would "tear your hide." During the Civil Rights Era, there was a huge population of baby boomers who had to navigate the social divide of their parents expectations and the discrimination heaped upon them outside of their community. Since there was no room for outward weakness in the face of chronic tragedy, coupled with the responsibility of representing the family name, for years they buried their grief and unanswered questions.

During my research, I was surprised to learn of the emotional detachment similarities I shared with other children of

Civil Rights leader's. In his book, *Children of the Movement*, John Blake interviewed the children of Dr. King, Malcolm X, Elijah Muhammad, Andrew Young, Stokely Carmichael, Julian Bond, Elaine Brown, and many others.[17]

Many of the children of the Movement received mixed messages from their parents, who were often absent due to arrests and their extended frontline activities. All of the leaders chose to keep their children out of the limelight. Ilysasah Shabazz, Malcolm X's daughter, did not really know anything about her father. After his assassination, her mother raised her and her sisters as a middle-class family. She attended private school only to learn in college the notoriety of her father's legacy. She read his book to become acquainted with his history and thoughts. Later she took a college course to learn more about him. Similarly, after the passing of my stepfather in 2016 and my mom in 2017, I was finally able to fully focus on my father's work. My knowledge about the Movement has vastly increased over the course of writing this book and subscribing to newspapers and magazine archives.

Ilyasha's story resonates with me on many levels. She often talks about the ache she feels for her father and how she avoided visiting his grave for many years. She also wondered what her life could have been if his life was not cut short during her childhood. I will be visiting my father's grave in February 2020. My sister and I have lived with the false narrative that he was cremated.

Similarly, Ilyasha states that the reality of losing her father hit her later in life. I am grieving all three of my parents at the same time. Their lives and their deaths are intertwined, and it is hard to grieve one and not the other. I might add that my stepdad is the recipient of all of the good feelings I attribute to any man because of the selfless dedication that Alfonso Duncan showed to my mom, my sister and me. His love and care for me is still the highest standard of excellence. He stepped in and stepped up to take care of a ready-made family and never looked back.

Although it may sound contrite, I have often wondered if I would have had a great relationship with my father. What if we didn't get along? What if he was more of a disciplinarian than Mr. Duncan? Daddy Duncan was a toy-fixer, boo boo kisser, and had the strength of three men. He taught me how to dance with my feet on top of his, how to ride a bike, even running behind me until I mastered it. He was a fierce watchman over his home and his three ladies. Perhaps my father would not have had the same level of patience or temperament. These conflicting thoughts recur often. If truth be told, in all of the historical pages about him, not one article mentions his family or children. Maybe it was for our safety, like other leaders in the Movement. *I want to believe that this is the case.* It's sad and nerve-wrecking at the same time, but at the end of the day, I will never know the answer.

Over the years, I've read studies touting the positive emotional and psychological benefits of girls who have close relationships with their dads. There's evidence that girls can handle everyday stressors better than girls without close relationships with fathers in the home, and they are less prone to depression and anxiety, and are better able to talk about their feelings.[18] Most girls model their male relationships with others based on their father's character, yet boys model themselves after their father's character. Boys seek approval from their fathers at an early age and begin to imitate their behaviors.

Like the other children of the Movement, Dexter King, son of Dr. Martin Luther King Jr. describes his life as being in a holding pattern because he did not have closure about his father's assassination. Although being the child of Dr. King has an enormous amount of pressure as a world hero, Dexter's inability to find closure resonates with many about their parents as heroes for the Movement. The gut-wrenching experience of not knowing the person or the truth travels to the heart and literally aches. These tears are different than tears of joy and have been shown to be different in their chemical composition.[19]

You would think that my tears would have dissipated by now. Especially since I have no recollection of my father. Yet each time I read about him or see his photo I cannot help but well up inside. Grief has so many dimensions and I am still learning how to channel and navigate this impactful legacy my father left on America.

As a middle-aged adult, I find myself in a club of daughters left fatherless during the 1960's. Some of them lost their fathers in the war. There was a large draft of Black men who fought in the Korean Conflict who died on the battlefield between 1950 -1953. Yet for those soldiers who survived they returned home to a segregated America where racial barriers were prominent in every area of life. Many fathers left home to find work and never returned creating other families elsewhere. [20] My mother could not bear my father being gone for long stretches early in the marriage as he sought legal work. Mom told Sheila and me, "Your father left us here because he couldn't pass the New Jersey Bar. I was tired of running up and down the road with him and I didn't go!" Who knows what my life would have been like had he passed the New Jersey Bar? I realize that everything happens for a reason and there was a much larger calling on my father's life in Virginia than in New Jersey.

CHAPTER 10

POWER TO THE PEOPLE

"Our grandfathers had to run, run,
run. My generation's out of breath.
We ain't running no more."
- Stokely Carmichael

A friend once stated, "You missed the revolution!" In many ways that was true. If anything, I was unaware of the significance of the Movement. My life was pretty sheltered in East Orange, New Jersey and I was focused on church and school activities. Yet my sister Sheila was down for the cause. In high school, she was made for the Movement and representing the Motherland. She sported the Angela Davis afro, dressed in African clothing and wore a gele. By the time she got to college, she admired Dr. King, yet was vocal on campus in her shared views with Malcolm X and Stokely Carmichael. Looking back, I didn't appreciate the church's role in the Movement but I was grounded in the faith.

I auditioned for a Broadway play, *Faith Journey*, for the role of an elderly church matron, "Sis Belle" and I was hired. It was my first audition and I could not believe that I landed the role the first time out. In hindsight, I was surrounded by women like Sis Belle all of my life. I worked full-time and my parents kept my children while I was on stage. I took the bus to New York City five nights a week for six months. It was a dream come true for me to be in a Broadway play and perform musically. In those days, my mom was supportive, but she wanted me to get a "real job" and not waste the money spent on college. Working in the play was where I first heard the names of martyrs in the Movement like Rev. George Lee, Lamar Smith, Emmett Till, Medgar Evers, Ralph Abernathy, and many others. I received a great review from the New York Times, Theater Review, by Ben Brantley:

"Clarencia Shade, as a feisty church matron, stands out with a shimmering interpretation of "Over My Head."

Faith Journey

The Early Civil Rights Movement, Set to Music

The play (at the Lamb's Theater), directed by Chuck Patterson from Mr. Cuthbertson's script, follows the increasing social engagement of the members of the Second Street Baptist Church in Montgomery from 1955 to 1964. The church's minister, Paul (Craig Anthony Grant), is at first reluctant to lead his congregation into protest. He's a preacher, he insists, not a politician.

FAITH JOURNEY Book by Clarence Cuthbertson; music by George Broderick; lyrics by Mr. Broderick and Mr. Cuthbertson; directed by Chuck Patterson; visuals by Elizabeth Bello, Leon Oliver and Nelsena Burt Spano; choreography by Barry Carrington; Presented by Elohim Unlimited, in association with Jesse L. DeVore Jr. At the Lamb's Theater, 130 West 44th Street, Manhattan. WITH: Craig Anthony Grant (Paul), Claude Jay (Amos), Loreal Steiner (Lucille), Claudette Evans (Traci), Jeff Benish (Policeman/ Jason), Clarencia Shade (Sister Bell), Henry C. Rawls (J.P.), Janet Weeden (Ruby) and Robert L. Evans (Brother). [21]

Life Imitates Art

In 1959, Lorraine Hansbury's drama, *A Raisin in the Sun*, was a critically acclaimed Broadway play that highlighted life of an African American family on the Southside of Chicago dealing with a dilemma that crossed paths with the Fair Housing Act. The play's premise featured the Younger family seeking to improve their life beyond segregation by buying a house in a white neighborhood in the Chicago suburbs. The family is at odds over how to spend proceeds of a $10,000 life insurance policy after the death of the family patriarch.

Many of the issues the Younger family were challenged with in this one room play are relevant today in regards to the societal challenges and injustices of being Black in America and family disagreements over how to spend money. In addition, the play's plot hinges on a white neighbor against Blacks in his neighborhood to the point that he offers to buy the Younger family out. This play has been recreated over the years and the original cast featured Sidney Poitier, Ruby Dee, Claudia McNeil, Lou Gossett Jr. and others.

When Hansberry was writing *A Raisin in the Sun*, she told her husband that she was "going to write a social drama about Negroes that will be good art."[22]Hansberry was the first Black woman to write a Broadway play and hired a Black director. This timeless classic ran for over 500 performances and toured internationally. There was also a film in 1961. Hansberry won a Tony Award for "best play" by the New York Drama Critics' Circle. Several versions of the play followed over the years and it continues to touch crowds around the globe.[23]

I believe the arts are a necessary part of remembering African American History. I applaud the younger generation's documenting the untold stories of greatness in our recorded history.

The school system skims over these stories that can't be ignored. They fail to fill in the gaps about African American achievements before the slave trade as well as those born free in Europe. It is necessary for African Americans to continue to take our history to the theater, small and big screen and our music to the masses. If we don't, no one else will.

PART II

RICHMOND'S JACKSON WARD DISTRICT

CHAPTER 11

STRIKING GOLD

"It always seems impossible until it's done."

Nelson Mandela

Years ago, it was difficult to find any information about my father. I often typed his name in search boxes in library computer databases and was disappointed when the familiar words, "Your Search Yielded No Results" appeared on the screen. I was determined to keep searching. Deep down I kept telling myself, *"no results"* just means *"no results yet."* Then out of the blue, after years of searching, I had a hit! My father was mentioned in *Blue Laws and Black Codes: Conflict, Courts, and Change in Twentieth-Century Virginia*, by Peter Wallenstein. My emotions were all over the place. On the one hand I was ecstatic. On the other hand, I was shocked and scared at what I might find. I followed the link, purchased the book and reached out to Mr. Wallenstein.

On Sun, Aug 25, 2013 at 2:44 PM, <clsshade@aol.com> wrote:

Dear Professor Wallenstein,

I would like to_thank you_for your research on my father's contribution to the civil rights movement of Virginia. Your work in your latest book Blue Laws, Black Codes, which I purchased opened up a world to me. I was age 6 when my father passed. My mother never shared this information with me or I was too young to grasp it. Do you have any additional historical documents, interviews research or pictures you could share with me and my sister? It would be a joy just to speak to you. I am my father's namesake (Clarencia). I grew up in New Jersey. I am willing to travel to you if necessary.

A few days later Professor Wallenstein responded that he would get back to me as he had been traveling and classes were soon to resume. In an email he thanked me for getting in touch with him about my father and that he is "always very happy to hear from someone whose father was the lawyer in a case, or whose grandfather brought the case, and the like." His words touched me and once again I was proud to be Clarence Newsome's daughter.

Walllenstein's mention lead to hundreds of articles, interviews, and other information about my father and the surrounding environment in Richmond.

I read and photocopied one document after the next with sheer excitement. It was as if I had literally struck gold. After years and years of digging, and coming up empty, I unearthed information that is more valuable to me than gold and will bring closure for me and my family, while benefitting society as a whole.

Inside Jackson Ward District

My father was part of the Black Wall Street of the South. The Jackson Ward District was known as the Harlem of the South in Richmond, Virginia. The Civil Rights Movement in Richmond was marked by the intense efforts of Jackson Ward lawyers, businessmen, professionals, and others to establish equitable treatment through integration, voter registration, and loyalty to the black-owned businesses. The movement's success was a result of a community of activists who organized and inspired others in meetings, sermons, and social gatherings that took place in historic downtown Richmond. My father was pictured in national and local newspapers a few times a week. The Afro-American Newspaper chronicled every aspect of the Movement. Some articles were local while others were regional covering the news of several states.

My father was a sharp dresser and always had a touch of his favorite color red in his ensemble. He was ultra-stylish and identified with the Hollywood Jet-set club in his taste and demeanor. He was known for wearing Ray-Ban sunglasses and magical dimples and his good looks could have landed him in a recurring role in Hollywood. I found an issue of *Jet Magazine,* March 1961, with a photo of my father at President Kennedy's inaugural ball. He is dressed in a tuxedo with his second wife, Thelma Gilpin Newsome. [24] My father definitely had "swag."

He was moving in the elite social circle of the Talented Tenth and was featured in *Jet* twice.

He also liked photography and tried his hand at double exposure photos. He created a double exposure of himself in his Army uniform as well as a photo of my sister Sheila with his thoughts inscribed in the background. In addition to photography, his other creative outlet was singing in the choir. He was multi-talented, with excellent written and communication skills. I also believe he was such a good lawyer because he loved history and was able to retain facts about the law and cases.

My father and several of his colleagues worked for the Legal Defense Fund of the NAACP. The Richmond Chapter was swelling with cases. There was even an anti-lynching platform to force the country to halt this barbaric act. Lynching was used to intimidate entire communities. It was a method that was not only effective in discouraging voter registration, but it also served as punishment for those who would challenge the social norms of looking or speaking to a white woman or standing up for their rights. It was 1954 when the *Brown vs the Board of Education* case shifted the landscape of the separate but equal, ending school segregation. My father was still serving in the Army in Berlin, Germany when the Brown case was decided. Years later, he would connect with the legal scholars from his alma mater, Howard University, who wrote and filed the brief for Brown, attorney's Spotswood W. Robinson and Oliver Hill. Hill formed the famous legal team of Hill, Tucker and Marsh of Richmond, Virginia and hired my father. Oliver Hill and my father were colleagues, and friends. Hill served as the best man in my father's second marriage.

I reached out to Margaret Edds, author of *We Face the Dawn: Oliver Hill, Spottswood Robinson, and the Legal Team that Dismantled Jim Crow*, to see if she had information on my father. She definitely recalled his name, but did not include him in her book. However, she provided invaluable research leads at the Library of Virginia where I found all of the copies of the Richmond Afro-American newspaper from the 1940s forward in microfilm.

During my research, I discovered that my father's home is listed on the National Register of Historic Places. His residence was located at 11 Clay Street East. All of the law firms and other professional offices in Jackson Ward are registered as historic places. I am grateful to the firm of Sadler & Whitehead Architects, PLC for providing a detailed inventory of buildings associated with the Civil Rights Movement from the Jackson Ward District as well as the significance and background of the location.[25]

NPS Form 10-900-a
(8-86)

OMB Approval No. 1024-0018

United States Department of the Interior
National Park Service

National Register of Historic Places
Continuation Sheet

Jackson Ward Historic District (Additional Documentation)
City of Richmond, Virginia

Section number ___7___ Page ___7___

AN INVENTORY OF BUILDINGS
IN THE JACKSON WARD HISTORIC DISTRICT
THAT ARE ASSOCIATED WITH THE CIVIL RIGHTS ERA

The three buildings whose status has changed from "non-contributing" to "contributing" are indicated with a double asterisk (**)

First Street, North
400 Block (Even)

420   ca.1880, Italianate, 2-story, brick residence converted to commercial use, stretcher bond, 2 bays, corbelled brick and molded cornice, rock-faced stone lintels, projecting bay, 1/1 windows, central chimney. Law offices of civil rights attorneys Roland Ealey, Herman Benn, and M. Ralph Page in the 1960s. In 1963, the Richmond Branch of the NAACP was located in the building.

Second Street, North
500 Block (Even)

516   ca. 1900, Italianate, 2-story, brick commercial building, stretcher bond, 2 bays, bracketed cornice, paired 1/1 windows, molded storefront cornice intact. Annex for the Hotel Harris, one of three African American hotels associated with North 2nd Street entertainment and nightlife during the 1940s and 1950s.

528   The Hippodrome Theatre, ca. 1934, Art Deco, 2-story, stucco, symmetrical façade, with paired central entry doors. This theater was a popular entertainment center from the 1930s through the 1950s. The Hippodrome attracted the "greats" of the era, including Duke Ellington, Billie Holiday, and Louis Armstrong.

500 Block (Odd)

537   ca. 1890, Italianate, 2-story, brick commercial building, stretcher bond, 4 bays, pilasters and cornice on storefront, 1/1 windows with segmental arches, bracketed cornice at roof line. Office of Benjamin A. Cephas Real Estate for over thirty years. Cephas was the first African American appointed to the Richmond Public Library Board.

539-541   Hotel Eggleston, ca. 1900, Italianate, 3-story, brick hotel, 6 bays, Permastone facing on second and third floors, metal balconies on second and third floors, 1/1 windows with segmental arches. Hotel owned by Neverett Eggleston, Sr. The Hotel Eggleston and its restaurant Neverett's Place were popular meeting spots for Richmond African Americans in the 1940s and 1950s.

NPS Form 10-900-a
(8-86)

OMB Approval No 1024-0018

**United States Department of the Interior
National Park Service**

**National Register of Historic Places
Continuation Sheet**

Section number __7__ Page __8__

**Jackson Ward Historic District (Additional Documentation)
City of Richmond, Virginia**

---

600 Block (Odd)

603   ca. 1900, Vernacular, 2-story, brick commercial building, stretcher bond, 4 bays, plain cornice. This building housed Richmond's premier African American photography firm, Brown's Photography.

Third Street, North
600 Block (Even)

614   Third St. Bethel AME Church, ca. 1857, Italianate, 1-story, 4 bays, 1-story front porch of brick and wood with a brick balustrade and Tuscan columns, lancet arch windows with tracery, corbeling and other decorative brickwork, towers on both front corners, gabled roof. One of Jackson Ward's most active churches in the Civil Rights movement. The church was the site for numerous organizational meetings.

Clay Street, East
1 Block (Odd)

11   ca. 1878, Italianate, 2-story, brick residence, stretcher bond, 3 bays, 1-story porch with iron posts, brackets, frieze and balustrade, 2/2 segmental-arch windows, decorative vents. Home of Clarence W. Newsome, civil rights attorney with the firm of Hill Tucker & Marsh.

100 Block (Even)

110-112**   The Virginia Mutual Benefit Life Insurance Company Building was designed by Tiffany Armstrong, architect with David Warren Harwicke & Partners. It was built in 1963 for community leaders and businessmen Booker T. Bradshaw and Clarence Townes, Sr. to house their insurance company business headquarters and other tenants, including the neighborhood ABC store. Until the mid-1990s when Jackson Center was built nearby on 2nd Street, this was the largest office building in Jackson Ward. The Virginia Mutual Beneficial Life Insurance Company Building, at the northwest corner of Second and Clay Streets, has one of the most prominent sites in Jackson Ward. The owners and their architect consciously rejected the idea of constructing a building in a traditional idiom. Their goal was to create a modern structure that would speak to the future rather than the past.

The building has the stripped-down aesthetic of the International Style. A four story rectangular box constructed of pre-cast concrete, the building is organized by windows aligned in the open vertical strips between the shallow projections of the U-shaped wall panels. The base of the building is clad with a slate veneer, except at the south-facing entry elevation. A wall of storefront doors and windows is recessed behind an arcade created by two square columns. Most of the building's interior has been altered over time due to the changes of business and retail tenants. The elevator lobbies are distinguished by beige and blue-green mosaic wall panels and,

NPS Form 10-900-a
(8-86)

OMB Approval No 1024-0018

United States Department of the Interior
National Park Service

National Register of Historic Places
Continuation Sheet

Section number   7   Page   9

Jackson Ward Historic District (Additional Documentation)
City of Richmond, Virginia

Clay Street, East, cont.

110-112**   at the small entry lobby a suspended ceiling of bronze and blue-green, anodized, aluminum
cont.   squares.

Virginia Mutual Benefit Life's founders were community leaders who supported the Civil Rights
Movement with significant financial contributions and business expertise.

200 Block (Even)

206-208**   Doctors Howlette and Thornton Medical Offices. Optometrist John Howlette, MD and podiatrist
            William S. Thornton hired architect C. Page Highfill of Hyland and Highfill architects in 1961 to
            design their offices at 206-208 East Clay Street. The project pairs long, narrow one-story
            buildings along a canopied walk. The buildings are brick boxes, designed in the modern style
            with very little ornament. Corrugated panels shelter the serpentine walk leading from the
            property's gated entry to an outdoor fountain centered between the two offices. The narrow
            garden lining this path is planted with topiary and other ornamental shrubs. The site presents an
            unexpected oasis in the city. The entry bay in each of the buildings is delineated with a wall
            panel of painted diagonal siding. In the case of this unusual property, these two understated
            buildings become a backdrop to the property's primary feature, its garden.

            John L. Howlette and William S. Thornton were both prominent doctors and community leaders.
            Thornton was one of the founding members of the Crusade for Voters.

212-214   Southern Aid Society of Virginia Building, ca. 1910, Renaissance Revival, office building, brick,
            stretcher bond, 4-story, 7 bays, first floor pediments, Corinthian pilasters, 1/1 windows with
            arches and keystones, rustication, cornice with modillions, parapet roof. Headquarters for the
            Southern Aid Life Insurance Company and numerous professional offices including the law firm
            of civil rights attorneys Hill Tucker & Marsh.

Clay Street, West
400 Block (Odd)

419   ca. 1883, Italianate, brick residence, stretcher bond, 2-story, 2 bay, brick stoop, pilasters and
            entablature around entrance, large bowed window, cornice with dentils and frieze with vents.
            Home of Earl W. Davis, a Field Representative for the CIO (Congress of Industrial
            Organizations) who was a leader in the Crusade for Voters.

OUTSPOKEN

NPS Form 10-900-a
(8-86)

OMB Approval No. 1024-0018

United States Department of the Interior
National Park Service

National Register of Historic Places
Continuation Sheet

Jackson Ward Historic District (Additional Documentation)
City of Richmond, Virginia

Section number ___7___ Page __10__

Clay Street, West cont.
500 Block (Odd)

503   ca. 1850, Greek Revival residence, brick, stretcher bond, 2-story on a raised basement, 3 asymmetrical bays, sidelights and transom at front door, Greek Revival porch with square posts, plain frieze and cornice, 6/6 windows, stepped parapet roof. Home of Roy West, community leader and Richmond Public Schools administrator during desegregation West served on the Richmond City Council and was elected Mayor in 1982.

Leigh Street, East
100 Block (Even)

102   ca. 1880, Italianate, brick residence, stretcher bond, 2-story, 3 bays, Neo-Classical porch with Corinthian columns and turned balustrade, 1/1 segmental-arch windows, bracketed cornice with decorative vents. Home of Dr. J.J. Smallwood, professor at Virginia Union University and active in the Civil Rights movement.

104   ca. 1880, Italianate, brick residence, stretcher bond, 2 story, 3 bays, porch with decorative iron posts, balustrade and brackets, cornice with modillions, shed roof. Home of James H. Johnston, President of Virginia State College, Petersburg, VA, who was active in the Civil Rights movement.

118   ca. 1880, Italianate, brick residence, stretcher bond, 2 story, 3 bays, stone stoop, 2/2 windows, full-length windows on the first floor, bracketed cornice with decorative vents. Law offices in late 1950s of civil rights attorneys Oliver Hill, Martin C. Martin, and James R. Olphin.

100 Block (Odd)

117   ca. 1880, Italianate, brick residence, stretcher bond, 2 story, 3 bays, Victorian Vernacular porch with turned posts and balustrade and sawn brackets, double front door, 2/2 segmental-arch windows, bracketed cornice with dentils and decorative vents. First Richmond law office (1939) of prominent civil rights attorney Oliver W. Hill.

Leigh Street, West
1 Block (Even)

12-14 **   Sheffield Building, ca. 1880 with 1965 addition, Italianate, brick office building, stretcher bond, 2 story, 7 asymmetrical bays, one-story section with fixed sash windows, 2/2 windows in two story section, bracketed cornice. James E. Sheffield moved his law practice to the Sheffield Building in 1965 as part of a larger effort to revitalize Jackson Ward. In 1974, Sheffield became the first African American Virginia Circuit Court judge.

NPS Form 10-900-a
(8-86)

OMB Approval No. 1024-0018

United States Department of the Interior
National Park Service

National Register of Historic Places
Continuation Sheet

Jackson Ward Historic District (Additional Documentation)
City of Richmond, Virginia

Section number __7__ Page __11__

Leigh Street, West, cont.

18   ca. 1890, Queen Anne, brick residence, stretcher bond, 2 story, 3 bays, Neo Classical porch with Corinthian columns and simple turned balustrade, 1/1 windows with rock-faced stone lintels, projecting turret, false mansard slate roof. Home of S.W. Robinson successful Jackson Ward real estate attorney.

216   Ebenezer Baptist Church, ca. 1858, Greek Revival, brick clad with stucco, Ionic columns form stone and brick portico, arched stained glass windows on sides, shingle roof with pediment gable, cupola with Palladian louvered vents and four spires, iron fence. The 1963 civil rights march on Richmond City Hall to draw attention to inequities in employment opportunities originated at this church.

St. James Street
500 Block (Even)

520   ca.1880, brick residence, stretcher bond, 2-story, 3 bays, Victorian Vernacular wood porch 3 bays wide with square posts and balustrade and sawn brackets, full length windows on first floor, 2/2 segmented-arch windows upstairs, bracketed cornice with decorative grills. Home of Dr. Joseph E. Jones, professor at Virginia Union University who was active in the Civil Rights movement.

NPS Form 10-900-a
(8-86)

OMB Approval No. 1024-0018

United States Department of the Interior
National Park Service

National Register of Historic Places
Continuation Sheet

Jackson Ward Historic District (Additional Documentation)
City of Richmond, Virginia

Section number __8__   Page __12__

8. STATEMENT OF SIGNIFICANCE

Jackson Ward, the historic heart of Richmond's African American community, was profoundly involved in and affected by the civil rights struggle. It was the locus from which dozens of desegregation cases were filed by the law firms of Hill Robinson & Martin, and later Hill Tucker & Marsh. The Ward served as an incubator for black businesses. Excluded from participation in white civic and business affairs, blacks developed interdependent relationships that gave rise to businesses whose success garnered political and economic clout to the black community. The business and political leadership nurtured in the Ward helped to unmake segregation.

Jackson Ward is significant on the national level under *National Register Criterion A* for its critical role in the Civil Rights movement. The Historic District meets *Criterion Consideration G* because of the broad significance of the Civil Rights movement in our nation's history. This extension of the district's period of significance, 1940 to 1970, begins at the time when Jackson Ward's civil rights strategy had matured among the black leaders and action resulted. The era continues through the years of the Civil Rights movement and ends in 1970, the year District Court Judge Robert R. Merhige handed down his landmark ruling that students would be bussed to achieve racial integration of public schools.

HISTORIC CONTEXT

Jackson Ward's Historic Designation

The Jackson Ward Historic District was listed on the Virginia Landmarks Register in April 1976 and the National Register of Historic Places in June 1978 because: "The area is broadly significant to students of black, urban, and business history and is unique for having been the center of Negro community life in Richmond during a watershed era for that race and the nation."[2] In June 1978, the exceptional significance of Jackson Ward was formally recognized when it was awarded National Historic Landmark status. The neighborhood was comprehensively surveyed by Tyler Potterfield with the City of Richmond and David Edwards of the Virginia Department of Historic Resources in 1987 and 1997. The 1976 Nomination Form authored by Margaret Peters, Calder Loth, H. Peter Pudner, and Joseph Yates, notes that the Period of Significance for the Jackson Ward Historic District extends from 1800 – 1899 and from 1900 (with no concluding year). This addendum proposes to specifically extend the period of significance to include the Civil Rights Era beginning in 1940 and to designate 1970 as the period's terminus.

Background

Segregation developed in Jackson Ward due to restrictive public policies and local attitudes concerning the rights of African Americans following the Civil War. By 1940, the Ward had become home to approximately 5000 African Americans. It was the heart of Richmond's black commercial, cultural, and religious life. In effect, Jackson Ward functioned economically and politically as a "separate city" within the larger metropolis. Following the example of Maggie Lena Walker and the reconstruction era organizations that grew out of the black churches and fraternal organizations, black citizens of the Civil Rights era continued to give back to

91

NPS Form 10-900-a
(9-86)

OMB Approval No. 1024-0018

**United States Department of the Interior
National Park Service**

**National Register of Historic Places
Continuation Sheet**

Section number ___8___ Page __13__

**Jackson Ward Historic District (Additional Documentation)
City of Richmond, Virginia**

strengthen their community. They took pride in their race, and ultimately banded together to overcome obstacles imposed by both legal segregation and the equally limiting *de facto*, or customary segregation.

Ironically, as monumental achievements were made by Jackson Ward attorneys litigating civil rights cases through the court system, Richmond's city planners forever altered the physical fabric of the community through an expansive urban renewal program. Residents could do little to influence the path of the proposed roads and Jackson Ward soon found itself bisected, both vertically and horizontally, by the broad concrete expanses of the I-95 expressway and the Belvidere Street extension. Though urban renewal removed some of the area's most blighted residential properties, it also demolished the physically cohesive community. By 1970, the impact of the city's urban renewal program and blacks' recently won civil rights became evident as many businesses closed or relocated. But even as the physical fabric was lost, the black community continued to identify with Jackson Ward. As a result, efforts to revitalize the neighborhood are underway so that the Ward can nurture another proud generation.

The years 1940 to 1970 represent an era of unprecedented black achievement as successful litigation brought the integration of public schools and African Americans were elected and appointed to numerous political and judicial positions for the first time in our nation's history.

Prominence in the fight for Civil Rights

Litigation
Jackson Ward was the locus from which dozens of desegregation cases were filed by the law firm of Hill Martin & Robinson, later Hill Tucker & Marsh. Senior partner Oliver W. Hill served as head of the National Association for the Advancement of Colored People's (NAACP) Virginia legal defense team. Over time the firm has operated out of several offices, all located within Jackson Ward. The initial thrust was to prove that the *Plessy v. Ferguson* (1896) decision, which had established 'separate but equal,' was unconstitutional. Hill and partner Spottswood W. Robinson III represented the plaintiff in the Prince Edward County desegregation case *Davis v. County School Board of Prince Edward County* (1951). This case became one of five that formed *Brown v. Board of Education of Topeka, Kansas* (1954). Hill and Robinson joined New York NAACP attorney Thurgood Marshall in successfully arguing *Brown v. Board of Education of Topeka, Kansas* before the United States Supreme Court, thus effectively ending legal school segregation.

Virginia's response to *Brown* was to create policies that collectively became known as "Massive Resistance." Hill's firm vigorously filed law suits opposing the legislature's efforts to perpetuate segregation. In a 1999 interview, Hill stated that suits were filed against Virginia school systems in sixty jurisdictions—representing more litigation than any other state in the Union.[3] Among the acts of Virginia's General Assembly were the Gray Plan (1956) that provided tuition for private school and empowered School Boards to determine pupil school placement and the Stanley Plan (1956) composed of thirteen actions designed to prevent integration. Hill and his legal team responded by filing cases against school boards in Arlington, Norfolk, Newport News, and Charlottesville. Before these cases could be settled, the General Assembly moved to establish independent Pupil Placement Boards. Within the year, Hill successfully obtained a court order temporarily stopping this practice in Richmond. However, the test came when, as the 1958 school year began, six African American

NPS Form 10-900-a
(8-86)

OMB Approval No 1024-0018

United States Department of the Interior
National Park Service

National Register of Historic Places
Continuation Sheet

Jackson Ward Historic District (Additional Documentation)
City of Richmond, Virginia

Section number __8__ Page __14__

students were denied placement in the all white school of their choice. Attorney Martin A. Martin (partner in Hill Martin and Robinson) represented the plaintiffs in this case *Warden v. Richmond School Board* (1958). Though no settlement was reached until 1961, success was achieved in August 1960 when two African American students were admitted to all white Chandler Elementary School.

Another Richmond School Board tactic to prevent integration was to create "dual attendance zones." Eleven African American parents filed a class action suit to challenge this procedure in *Bradley v. Richmond School Board* (1961). Attorneys Samuel W. Tucker and Henry Marsh III of Hill Tucker & Marsh successfully argued this case and in 1963 the Freedom of Choice Plan was established. However, few students chose to attend a school outside of their district and due to Richmond's segregated residential patterns, schools remained segregated. Tucker and Marsh filed the pivotal case leading to Judge Robert R. Merhige, Jr.'s 1970 landmark ruling in which he ordered the bussing of black and white students to schools outside of their neighborhoods in order to stimulate racial integration of public schools. The ruling would have a profound effect on Jackson Ward and on the nation at large.

Civil rights cases originating from the offices of Jackson Ward attorneys were not limited to school desegregation. Three other examples involved public school teachers' salaries, courtroom seating, and segregation of restaurants. In 1941, Hill teamed with fellow NAACP attorneys Leon Ransom, District of Columbia, and Thurgood Marshall, New York, to represent the black Richmond Teacher's Association in obtaining black teacher salaries equal to those paid white teachers. Immediately upon hearing the suit had been filed, the Richmond School Board passed a pay parity plan. In 1963, the firm of Ealey & Page successfully represented the plaintiff before the U.S. Supreme Court whereby the Court ruled that segregated seating in courtrooms was unconstitutional. The offices of attorneys Roland D. Ealey, and M Ralph Page were located at 420 N. 1st Street (JWHD, NHL)[4]. Also in 1963, Hill associate Clarence W. Newsome represented student demonstrators who had been arrested during a lunch counter demonstration.

Voter Registration
Litigation was but one tool used by Richmond's African American population to gain their civil rights; voter registration was a second method. In 1936, only 1,527 blacks were registered to vote. Increasing this number was difficult as many blacks felt their vote did not count. By 1940, through efforts of Jackson Ward dentist Jesse M. Tinsley, President of the Richmond branch NAACP, and Roscoe C. Jackson of the Democratic Voter's League, the number of blacks voting rose by 50 percent. The progressive mayoral candidate Gordon B. Ambler won, with the support of the black vote. During his administration, he began to address long-standing community problems. The power of the vote was not lost on Richmond's black citizens and in 1948 they helped elect attorney Oliver W. Hill as the first African American to serve on the City Council since Reconstruction.

In the wake of *Brown,* Virginia's legislature mounted an offense against both school integration and the organizations that fought for integration—particularly the NAACP. In 1956, the Richmond Crusade for Voters was founded to sustain the NAACP's efforts in registering voters. Founders were William S. Thornton, John Mitchell Brooks, and William Fergusen Reid. The Crusade's voter-registration campaign during 1957 was known as the "Miracle of Richmond." The drive resurrected an antebellum tradition whereby one black taught

NPS Form 10-900-a
(8-86)

OMB Approval No. 1024-0018

United States Department of the Interior
National Park Service

National Register of Historic Places
Continuation Sheet

Jackson Ward Historic District (Additional Documentation)
City of Richmond, Virginia

Section number __8__ Page __15__

---

another to read. The motto "each one teach one" now became "each one reach one." The highly successful campaign resulted in a 30 percent increase in black voter registration by 1958.[5] Alarmed by the success of the voter registration campaigns, the Virginia legislature introduced "blank sheet" registration under the guise of testing literacy. The *Richmond Afro-American, the Richmond Planet* countered from its offices at 301 E. Clay Street (now demolished) by launching a "Boomerang for Bigots" program aimed at educating blacks on how to fill in the blank form thus lessening the impact of the blank sheet registration maneuver.[6]

The organizational minds behind the Crusade were educated black professionals who met daily in strategy sessions. Many meetings were held at Slaughters Hotel at 527-529 North 2nd Street (now demolished) and later at the 533 Club next door (now demolished). The commitment was substantial since the Crusade's goal was not only to register voters, but also provide voter education, endorse candidates, establish precinct clubs, and provide transportation to the polls. By the 1962 city council elections, the Crusade had become so effective that seven of the nine candidates it endorsed were elected. In 1966, African Americans represented 48 percent of Richmond's population and 34 percent of all registered voters.

Critical to the voter registration and other civil rights campaigns were the city's black churches—fifteen of which were located in Jackson Ward. These churches, particularly Fifth Street Baptist Church, 705 N. 5th Street (now demolished), Third Street Bethel African Methodist Episcopal, 616 N. 3rd Street (NRHP)[7], and Leigh Street African Methodist Episcopal, 500 E. Leigh Street (now demolished) were the location for mass meetings. But all churches were critical to the effort, with their pastors playing key rolls.

Non-violent protest

Both the Richmond Branch and Virginia Chapter of the NAACP had their offices in Jackson Ward. NAACP staff worked zealously with professors and students at Virginia Union University, pastors, and local businessmen in organizing civil rights protests. Individual actions also garnered attention. As early as 1939, local NAACP president Jesse Tinsley and his wife Ruth defied Richmond's social conventions by entertaining First Lady Eleanor Roosevelt in their home at 531 N. 4th Street (now demolished).[8] Richmond's first organized protest occurred in February 1960 when students from Virginia Union University staged the first "sit-in" at F. W. Woolworth's lunch counter. Other lunch counters targeted included G. C. Murphy, Thalhimer's, and Peoples Service Drug. Later, while picketing Thalhimer's department store, three blacks were arrested. Those arrested included Ruth Tinsley, whom though not picketing was standing near the store and refused to comply with a police officer's order to "move on." By June 1963, sixty restaurants had dropped racial barriers. Demonstrations continued through the year. In August, picketers marched from Ebenezer Baptist Church, 216 W. Leigh Street (JWHD, NHL), down Broad Street to demand increased job opportunities within city government. And later, between 300 and 400 demonstrators gathered at the black YMCA, 214 E. Leigh Street (now demolished), for a bus caravan to D.C. to join the March on Washington.

Richmond's demonstrations differed from those in other states in that they proceeded with few arrests and without violence. But Richmond had not been a passive player in the Civil Rights movement. It has been suggested that the leaders of Richmond's Civil Rights movement were primarily conservative businessmen who had learned to work within the system and who had confidence in achieving the goal through legal means. [9] What is evident is that local black leaders were effective in devising strategies that achieved the desired

NPS Form 10-900-a
(8-86)

OMB Approval No. 1024-0018

United States Department of the Interior
National Park Service

National Register of Historic Places
Continuation Sheet

Jackson Ward Historic District (Additional Documentation)
City of Richmond, Virginia

Section number ___8___ **Page** __16__

outcome without provoking violence. Their actions contributed significantly to passage of the Civil Rights Act of 1964 and the Voting Rights Act of 1965. Important local successes resulting from their efforts are the "firsts" for African Americans who worked and lived in Jackson Ward.

1948 - Oliver W. Hill became first African American elected to the Richmond City Council since Reconstruction

1953 - Booker T. Bradshaw elected as first African American on the Richmond School Board

1964 - Spottswood W. Robinson, III became first African American appointed as a judge on the U.S. District Court in Washington. In 1966, Robinson became first African American appointed to the U.S. Court of Appeals for the District of Columbia.

1964 - Dr. William Ferguson Reid and Dr. William M.T. Forrestor became the first African Americans admitted to the Richmond Academy of Medicine

1964 - Benjamin A. Cephas became first African American appointed to the Board of the Richmond Public Library

1966 - William Ferguson Reid became first African American elected to General Assembly in modern times

1966 - Henry Marsh III elected to the City Council and in 1977 became Richmond's first African American Mayor

1974 - James E. Sheffield appointed as first African American Virginia Circuit Court Judge

Prominence of the Business Community

The Jackson Ward business community, with Second Street as its heart, developed as a result of local African Americans' determination to preserve their access to goods and services even as the white community was busy erecting Jim Crow laws to limit such access. Early key businesses, such as Maggie Walker's St. Luke's Penny Savings Bank (NRHP, NHL), and the Southern Aid Society (JWHD, NHL), had grown out of fraternal organizations and self-help societies with ties to the black church. By example, these institutions established a precedent–that business owners would give back, reinvest in their community. This commitment is clearly noted in the financial support and organizational acumen that businessmen provided to the Civil Rights movement.[10] It is also seen through the expansion of individual businesses that reinvested in the physical fabric of Jackson Ward by building new structures and redeveloping old.

Coupled with a business's obligation to the community was the black consumer's responsibility to support local black establishments. Local pastor Dr. Gordon Blaine Hancock, Moore Street Baptist Church, noted that because blacks "possessed little political clout, national, state, and local governments could ignore their complaints... By spending where possible in Negro enterprises, the Negro could at least provide jobs for some members of his group and, at the same time, use his leverage as a consumer to coerce white merchants to hire Negroes."[11] Dr. Hancock coined the phrase "Double Duty Dollar" to express this concept. Similar economic solidarity campaigns of the time included the NAACP's "Buy Black", frequently advanced in the black newspaper the *Afro-American and Richmond Planet*, and "Don't Buy Where You Can't Work."[12] The emphasis on taking pride in and reinvesting in one's race became for many a natural thought pattern and

NPS Form 10-900-a
(8-86)

OMB Approval No. 1024-0018

United States Department of the Interior
National Park Service

National Register of Historic Places
Continuation Sheet

Jackson Ward Historic District (Additional Documentation)
City of Richmond, Virginia

Section number __8__ Page __17__

---

ensured a vibrant, supportive community even as daily experiences resulting from Richmond's staunch segregationist policies were severely limiting.

For the black business owner, profitability remained a challenge, as black businessmen had to overcome competition from white business owners, who frequently had both the capital and credit to offer wider selection and better prices, and also an increasingly blighted streetscape created by overcrowding and poverty within the Ward.[13] In spite of these challenges, black owned businesses in Jackson Ward, and particularly along 2nd Street, thrived. Few consumer needs would have gone unfulfilled as businesses included established insurance and financial institutions, the offices of emerging young professionals, funeral parlors, real estate offices, hotels, restaurants, clubs, theaters, and service providers including barber and beauty shops, repair shops, dry cleaners and tailors. Residents remember the Jackson Ward of the 1940s and 1950s as "jumpin" and never closing.

Among Jackson Ward's established insurance companies were Richmond Beneficial Life Insurance and Southern Aid. In keeping with the self-help tradition, two insurance men Booker T. Bradshaw and Clarence Townes Sr. established the Virginia Mutual Benefit Life Insurance Company in 1933; with headquarters in the Southern Aid Building at 214 E. Clay Street (JWHD, NHL). Over the next thirty years their business thrived and expanded to Washington D.C. and other Virginia cities. In the early 1960s plans were developed for a new headquarters building. Desirous of being a positive force within the Jackson Ward community, Bradshaw and Townes purchased property prominently located on the corner of Second and Clay Streets for their building and employed progressive Richmond architect Tiffany Armstrong. At a time when Jackson Ward's commercial center was declining, Bradshaw and Townes gave Armstrong instructions to design a building that conveyed their faith in Jackson Ward's viability as a commercial center. The Virginia Mutual Benefit Insurance Building at 110-112 E. Clay Street was built in 1963 and remains a symbol of the achievements that earned Jackson Ward the reputation as "the Black Wall Street" in the 1900s. Its founders were leaders in the community serving on numerous boards. Their individual achievements include Mr. Bradshaw's election to the Richmond School Board in 1953, the first African American to serve in that capacity since Reconstruction, and Mr. Townes being cited by President Eisenhower for his service to the Department of Commerce's Advisory Committee on Minority Business Development.

Prominent financial institutions included the Consolidated Bank and Trust, successor to Maggie Walker's St. Luke's Penny Savings Bank. In 1966, Consolidated's president J. Jay Nickens, Jr. co-founded the Richmond Improvement Coordinating Council. The Council, noting that 75 percent of Richmond's black population was low income and unskilled, assisted these individuals, through education, to obtain better jobs and housing conditions. In current times, Consolidated continues to exert influence in the Jackson Ward community from its prominent building at 327-329 N. 1st Street (constructed in 1974, after the proposed period of significance).

During the Civil Rights era, numerous young black professionals established practices in Jackson Ward. Because Virginia colleges would not admit African Americans to their graduate programs, many students had received tuition assistance from the legislature to study out of state. They now returned and began dismantling the system that had enabled a segregated society. Most prominent among these was Oliver W. Hill who established a law practice with Spottswood W. Robinson III and Martin C. Martin in 1943. Their firm Hill Robinson & Martin was located first in the Consolidated Bank & Trust Building at 327 N. 1st Street

NPS Form 10-900-a
(8-86)

OMB Approval No. 1024-0018

United States Department of the Interior
National Park Service

National Register of Historic Places
Continuation Sheet

Jackson Ward Historic District (Additional Documentation)
City of Richmond, Virginia

Section number __8__   Page __18__

(demolished) and later at 623 N. 3rd Street (demolished). During the 1960s, when Samuel W. Tucker and Henry L. Marsh III joined forces with Hill, their firm Hill Tucker & Marsh was located in the Southern Aid Building at 214 E. Clay Street (JWHD, NHL). In addition to these firms' monumental success in litigating desegregation cases, the individual attorneys also achieved prominence. S. W. Robinson became the first African American to be appointed a judge on the U.S. District Court in Washington (1964). Later he was the first African American judge on the U.S. Court of Appeals for the District of Columbia (1966). In 1977, Henry Marsh III was elected as Richmond's first black mayor. In 1999, Oliver Hill was awarded the Presidential Medal of Freedom in recognition for his role as one of the "lions" of the Civil Rights movement. [14] In 2000, Hill received the American Bar Association's highest award in recognition for his leadership in the Civil Rights movement. [15]

Attorney James E. Sheffield, moved to Jackson Ward in 1965 when he chose to become part of the area revitalization effort. He purchased a vacant and dilapidated building at 12 - 14 West Leigh Street to house his law practice. The redevelopment project expanded the structure toward the street to accommodate additional office space. Other professional offices relocating to the Sheffield Building following this remodeling were those of attorney Harrison Bruce, physician Charles Cummings, and dentist Anthony Malloy. In 1974, attorney Sheffield became the first African American to be appointed as a Circuit Court Judge in Virginia.

Among the notable doctors and dentists establishing a practice in Jackson Ward were podiatrist William S. Thornton, optometrist John L. Howlette, physician William Fergusen Reid, and dentist Jesse M. Tinsley. Dr. Thornton and Dr. Howlette established their practices at 415 North 2nd (now demolished) in the 1950s. Throughout their lifetimes they worked to create opportunities for African Americans. Dr. Thornton, co-founder of the Crusade for Voters in 1956, served as its president for many years. Dr. Howlette, the second African American to be licensed to practice optometry in Virginia, in 1968 helped co-found the predominantly black National Optometric Association. Their ongoing commitment to the community was demonstrated in 1963 when they jointly invested in the construction of a modern office building at 206 - 208 East Clay Street. The prominent Richmond architectural firm of Hyland and Hyfill designed the building—a striking one-story structure with landscaped courtyard.

Also active in civil rights activities were Doctors Reid and Tinsley. William Fergusen Reid had joined Thornton and Brooks in founding the Crusade for Voters in the 1950s. In 1967, Dr. Reid was elected as the first African American to serve in the Virginia House of Delegates. Dr. Reid's office was located at 611 Chamberlayne Ave. (demolished). Jesse M. Tinsley served as president of the Richmond branch NAACP for fifteen years and then as state NAACP president for twenty years. Dr. Tinsley's dental practice at 402½ N. 2nd Street (outside JWHD) also housed the headquarters of the Richmond NAACP.

Due to a large and concentrated black population, service businesses also thrived during this era. The 1940 Hill's *Richmond City Directory* identifies 107 black retail or service related businesses along the streets of 1st, 2nd, 3rd, Clay and Leigh. This large number does not include those businesses that were operated out of an individual's home and thus were not given a listing. In some instances a business formed overnight when a local segregated practice created a need within the community. Such was the case of the Manhattan Car for Hire company, which seven men formed when white owned cab companies refused to pick-up black passengers. The business, using the owner's personal black Packards, operated out of 520 North 2nd Street

NPS Form 10-900-a
(8-86)

OMB Approval No. 1024-0018

United States Department of the Interior
National Park Service

National Register of Historic Places
Continuation Sheet

Jackson Ward Historic District (Additional Documentation)
City of Richmond, Virginia

Section number ___8___ Page ___19___

(demolished) from 1927 through the 1950s. Cab company executive Edward L. Slade, Jr. served as president of the Richmond Branch NAACP in the 1960s and was instrumental in organizing the bus caravan of demonstrators to the 1963 Civil Rights March on Washington.

Central to the social life of Jackson Ward were the theaters, restaurants, clubs, and hotels along the three blocks of N. 2nd Street between Clay and Leigh Streets. Interviews relate that "Two Street" never closed during the World War II years, as patrons and soldiers on leave would cross back and forth going from club to club, to the Hippodrome theater, and to restaurants and hotels. The Hippodrome booked the big entertainers of the time, including Duke Ellington, Billie Holiday, Nat King Cole, and Louis Armstrong, who then stayed at a 2nd Street hotel. In Richmond, only hotels located in Jackson Ward were open to African Americans. Most prominent of these were Slaughters (now demolished), Eggleston (JWHD, NHL), and Harris (now demolished).

Neverett Eggleston, owner of the Eggleston Hotel at 539 - 541 North 2nd Street, began his career by first managing the hotel when it was Miller's Hotel and then purchasing it. While making his hotel and its restaurant, Neverett's Place, one of the favorite spots along 2nd Street, he continued to purchase and develop commercial property in Jackson Ward. In 1954, he extensively remodeled the Eggleston Hotel creating a new facade in keeping with the modern architecture of the time. Neverett Eggleston, Jr. continued in his father's footsteps by investing in property and in 1964 built Motel Eggleston at 604 - 606 North 2nd Street. A third major property owner of the era was James R. Stallings who developed both housing and commercial properties. Stallings purchased his first house in the 1940s. In addition to rental housing, he invested in historic commercial properties purchasing the Hippodrome, St. Luke's Building, and Slaughter's Hotel as they became available. Stallings also constructed numerous new buildings in Jackson Ward, including apartments and retail space.

As an African American community, Jackson Ward has influenced thoughts and events far beyond its borders. When the number of African Americans purchasing property and establishing businesses grew in the 1900s, Jackson Ward became known as a black financial and entertainment center. The combination of successful businesses, influential churches, and fraternal organizations created an atmosphere in which educated black professionals could challenge Jim Crow laws and change history. Jackson Ward attorneys and businessmen not only participated in the Civil Rights movement, but were leaders in the key areas of litigation and voter registration. These achievements and the ongoing commitment of Richmond's African American citizens to Jackson Ward are recognized in this National Register Historic District amendment.

NPS Form 10-900-a
(8-86)

OMB Approval No. 1024-0018

**United States Department of the Interior
National Park Service**

**National Register of Historic Places
Continuation Sheet**

**Jackson Ward Historic District (Additional Documentation)
City of Richmond, Virginia**

Section number ___9___ Page ___20___

BIBLIOGRAPHY

American Bar Association. "Civil Rights Lawyer Oliver W. Hill to Receive 2000 American Bar Association Medal." News Release. Available from Internet at http://www.abanet.org.

Gavins, Raymond. *The Perils and Prospects of Southern Black Leadership: Gordon Blaine Hancock, 1884-1970.* Durham: Duke University Press, 1977.

Hill Directory. *Richmond, Virginia.* Richmond: Hill Directory Co., 1934, 1940, 1950, 1954, 1963,1970.

Loth, Calder and Margaret T. Peters. National Register of Historic Places Nomination Form for the Jackson Ward Historic District, Virginia Historic Landmarks Commission, 1976.

Luetjen, Karen Holt. "Second Street: Business and Entertainment in Jackson Ward 1900-1965." Manuscript. The Valentine Richmond History Center, Richmond, Va., 1990.

National Trust for Historic Preservation. "America's 11 Most Endangered Historic Places 2001-Historic Jackson Ward." Available from the Internet at http://www.nationaltrust.org/11Most/2001/jacksonwrd.htm.

Pratt, Robert A. *The Color of Their Skin: Education and Race in Richmond, Virginia 1954-1989.* Charlottesville: University Press of Virginia, 1993.

"Richmond Crusade for Voters Archives 1953-1995" Special Collections and Archives Department, James Branch Cabell Library, Virginia Commonwealth University, Richmond, Va., n.d.

Richmond Free Press. "Remembering a Heroine: Ruth E. Nelson Tinsley: A Strong Partner in the Civil Rights Movement." 17-19 February 1994.

Silver, Christopher and John V. Moeser. *The Separate City: Black Communities in the Urban South 1940-1968.* Lexington: University Press of Kentucky, 1995.

Townes, Clarence Jr. Interview by Kathryn E. Colwell. Richmond, Va., 15 March 2002.

Tyler-McGraw, Marie. *At the Falls: Richmond, Virginia, & It's People.* Chapel Hill, N.C.: University of North Carolina Press, 1994.

Williams, Michael Paul. "Rights Lion to get Medal of Freedom." *The Richmond Times Dispatch.* 22 May 1999.

_____. "Rights Push Here Strong, Not Stormy." *The Richmond Times Dispatch.* 14 March 1999.

Clarence Newsome graduation photo, photography hobby: double exposure photo, and Army uniform.

CHAPTER 12

THE RICHMOND 34

Randolph v. Commonwealth, 202 Va. 661 (1961)

*"Special emergency trespassing statutes
enacted recently by the General Assembly
aren't worth the paper they are written
on from a legal point of view."*
- ***Clarence W. Newsome***

My father was an attorney with the law offices of Hill, Tucker, and Robinson during the height of Jim Crow Laws. Oliver Hill formed the firm in 1948 and committed his practice to eradicating segregation. From 1948-1960 Hill, his partners, and their team of lawyers filed more civil rights lawsuits than any of the other southern states combined. The courage of the African American lawyers like my father across the country is well documented. They were grossly underpaid and spent hours traveling to wherever work was available, leaving their families behind for weeks at a time.

When Oliver Hill first started out, he made $10 a month. With this type of income, it was obvious that these civil rights leaders and activists believed in their cause to confront the Jim Crow system head on and faced danger including death at the hands of segregationist committed to preserving white supremacy.[26]

At the time, sit-downs were happening across the country. In addition to my father's working at Oliver Hill's firm, he was also Chairman of the Redress Committee of Richmond's NAACP branch. Frank Pinkston and Charles Sherrod were VUU students who formed the Richmond Movement. They met with my father at 4PM on February 19, 1960 to discuss the sit-down and the viability of non-violent protests by a customer. My father told them that they might be arrested, but he would handle their case.[27] After that conversation, the students of the Richmond Movement began protesting and boycotting stores in Downtown Richmond. During that time, Downtown Richmond was a premier shopping area. Blacks could shop in stores and spend their money, but they could not sit down to eat at the restaurants or in-store food counters. Blacks could not try on clothes, nor return clothing if it did not fit.[28]

On February 20, more than 200 VUU students marched from the campus to the downtown shopping district and sat down in white only areas until stores closed. This all happened without incident. A few days later, February 22, 1960, Raymond Randolph, Jr. and thirty-three of his VUU classmates were convicted of trespass when they boldly marched down Lombardy Street to Broad Street to Thalhimers Department Store in a peaceful demonstration of pride, dignity and respect.

Mr. Randolph and the other young men were dressed in shirts and ties and the young women wore dresses and heels. Thalhimers had a restaurant on the fourth floor for "whites only" and had lunch counters on the first floor for "whites only" and a lunch counter in the basement for Blacks. Mr. Randolph went to the fourth floor restaurant for service while the students attempted to obtain service at the first floor lunch counter. Mr. Randolph and the students were refused service because of their race. As a result of the VUU students arrest at Thalhimers Department Store on February 22, 1960, my father's legal acumen became widely known in the state of Virginia and elsewhere.

The facts in this landmark U.S. Supreme Court case, the store manager asked Randolph to leave the fourth floor or he would issue a warrant for his arrest. Randolph did not respond and remained in his position. Likewise, the other students did not respond when asked to leave and remained at the counter. Randolph and all 33 students were arrested for violation of Code 1950, section 18-225, which deems it a misdemeanor to remain on another's premises after having been forbidden to do so by the owner or custodian.[29] The students were carted off in six patrol wagons, arrested and charged with trespass. They were ordered to pay $20 fines. Little did they know that the community rallied behind them and donated what they could spare to ensure that all of the students' fines were paid. As a result of The Richmond 34 arrests, the students launched "The Campaign for Human Dignity" and VUU and high school students boycotted Downtown Richmond.[30] A few months later,

Downtown Richmond retailers had succumbed to the pressure of the boycott, and desegregation of Downtown Richmond retailers had begun. The Campaign for Human Dignity was successful, but the legal battle was far from over.

"The protesting Negroes have a precedent to stand on."
- Clarence W. Newsome

Oliver Hill wrote the brief to the Virginia Supreme Court for a writ of error for each of the 34 stating that the lower court erred in ruling against the students. My father and attorney Martin A. Martin argued on behalf of Randolph and the VUU students. Unfortunately, the court sustained the judgment of the lower court. The court held that there was sufficient evidence that the students violated the statute, and there was no evidence to support that the students were arrested because of their race. At that time, the Commonwealth had tried several other trespassing cases that were cited by the state that were also upheld.[31] The statute reads in full as follows:

> "| 18-225. Trespass after having been forbidden to do so. -- If any person shall without authority of law go upon or remain upon the lands or premises of another, after having been forbidden to do so by the owner, lessee, custodian or other person lawfully in charge of such land, or after having been forbidden to do so by sign or signs posted on the premises at a place or places where

they may be reasonably seen, he shall be deemed guilty of a misdemeanor, and upon conviction thereof shall be punished by a fine of not more than one hundred dollars or by confinement in jail not exceeding thirty days, or by both such fine and imprisonment."[32]

My father and his colleague, Martin A. Martin, were not deterred by the Virginia Supreme Court ruling. They knew they had another angle and believed they had a legitimate shot taking this case to the United States Supreme Court. In their brief, one of their arguments was that the Virginia trespassing statute as applied to the circumstances of this case was a denial of Randolph and the other student's rights granted under the Fourteenth Amendment of the U.S. Constitution. The Fourteenth Amendment granted citizenship and equal protection of laws to African Americans and slaves in 1868. Since the store was open during normal business hours to the public, Mr. Randolph and the other students were "business invitees." Therefore, denying them service based on race or color was a denial of their constitutional rights.

What's interesting about the Randolph case is that several other cases with a similar Fourteenth Amendment argument had been made in other jurisdictions, and all had been rejected.[33] It is "well settled that, although the general public have an implied license to enter a retail store, the proprietor is at liberty to revoke this license at any time as to any individual, and to eject such individual from the store if he refuses to leave when requested to do so."[34]

"These laws very soon will be tested sooner than you think.
Courts have held that a private company cannot
discriminate against persons if it has invited
those persons onto its premises."
- **Clarence W. Newsome**

As fate would have it, neither my father nor Martin A. Martin were aware of their U.S. Supreme Court victory which ruled sit-in arrests such as The Richmond 34 were illegal and unconstitutional. My father was too ill to be advised of this victory as he had been admitted to the hospital two days after attending the funeral of his friend and colleague, Martin A. Martin who died of a heart attack.

On the Front Line

The Richmond 34 trespassing arrest for sitting at the Thalhimers Department Store white only lunch counters were spawned out of the courage of the students from North Carolina A&T State University in Greensboro,who sat at a Woolworth's lunch counter a few weeks prior in nonviolent protests. Among those arrested were Joe Simmons and LaVerne Byrd Smith, and Elizabeth Johnson-Rice who have provided their stories over the years to the press.

In an interview years later, Simmons recalled how VUU's then President, Dr. Proctor warned him and others to represent VUU well and Dr. Proctor gave all 200 students his blessings.[35] Although LaVerne Smith did not participate in the sit-in, she was one of the picketers outside the Thalhimers Department store. Smith was part of the group that made the signs and set up the picket lines.[36] She was proud of her work and proud of the efforts of the VUU students. Smith also mentioned being called the "N" word as a four-year old by a white woman who refused to sit next to her. That incident left confusion and a sting in Smith's life and she wanted to become a lawyer to change the laws. Smith ultimately became a school teacher.[37]

Elizabeth Johnson-Rice was an active member of the Student Nonviolent Coordinating Committee and the Southern Christian Leadership Conference, and intended to be a spectator that day, but she and her brother were proud to be swept up into the protest. [38] She remembers being fearful of the German Shepherd dogs whose nose touched her leg. Elizabeth decided to stay focused and concentrate on something. To her surprise she remembered staring at the apple pie which was 25 cents a slice. After their arrest and fingerprinting, she recalls the crowd cheering them on outside the Eggleston Hotel. Johnson-Rice spotted her parents and realized they were proud of her and not angry that she participated in the protests.

The Richmond 34 Expungement: 2019

It's hard to believe that after 59 years, the criminal records from the Feb. 22, 1960, arrests of the Richmond 34 was expunged in February 2019. Although the charges were dismissed in 1965, it was not until 2018 that one of the students, Dr. Franklin, a professor at Boston College, realized the grave mistake.

Each of the 34 students was supposed to complete detailed paperwork and provide copies of their arrest record and other identification to wipe the record clean. Dr. Franklin applied for an expedited application for a Global Entry program and was denied by U.S. Customs because of his 1960 arrest. None of the students were aware that dismissal of the charges did not erase their arrest record. Fortunately, this detail has been corrected for all parties involved.

CHAPTER 13

JUSTICE FOR ALL

Boynton v. Virginia, 364 U.S. 454 (1960)

*"Every man of humane convictions must decide on the protest
that best suits his convictions, but we must all protest."*
- Dr. Martin Luther King, Jr.

Each time I read of my father's hard work and victories I felt more proud of his legacy. But when I read that he was friends with Thurgood Marshall and was one of the attorneys on the brief for the Boynton landmark interstate travel case, I was awestruck. Marshall argued the case, but my father, Martin A. Martin, Jack Greenberg, Louis A. Pollak, and Constance Baker Motley wrote the briefs.

I was three years old when my dad was working on the Boynton case. In an interview with attorney Henry Marsh and former Richmond Mayor, Julian Bond asked Marsh about the Boynton case. "He stopped in Richmond, and they tried to segregate him and he wouldn't move. He wouldn't use the black facility. And they arrested him. He called Oliver Hill and then they called Clarence Newsome because Oliver wasn't available at the time, and they represented him. That became the case that led to the Freedom Rides."[39]

In this case, Boynton was a Howard University law student traveling from Washington, D.C. to Alabama on a Trailways bus. When the bus arrived in Richmond, Virginia, the driver advised passengers that there would be a forty minute layover. Boyton entered the D.C. bus terminal to get a bite to eat. He went to the restaurant that had segregated seating. Boynton sat in the white only seating and requested a sandwich and a cup of tea. The waitress asked him to move to the other side of the restaurant and he refused. She then got a manager who advised him that he would be served on the other side. Boynton refused and was arrested, tried, convicted, and fined $10 dollars for violation of the same trespassing statute as The Richmond 34.[40]

Boynton was a Freedom Rider. These were groups of white and African American civil rights activists who protested segregated bus stations and tooks routes through the South on Greyhound and Trailways. They intentionally sat in "white only" areas at lunch counters and entered "white only" restrooms at terminals throughout the South. Freedom Riders were met with arrests and extreme violence from white protestors. U.S. Representative John Lewis was one of the original group of 13 Freedom Riders and he and other members were attacked in Rock Hill, South Carolina. The Freedom Riders endured bloody violence and at one point escaped a burning bus in Alabama that was bombed by over 200 white protestors surrounding the bus.[41]

Boynton appealed and argued that his conviction violated the Interstate Commerce Act and the Equal Protection Due Process and Commerce Clauses of the Federal Constitution, however the Virginia Supreme Court upheld his conviction. Then Thurgood Marshall and his legal dream team, filed a writ of certiorari. A "certiorari" is a Latin term which means "to be more fully informed." Marshall was granted the writ of certiorari which orders a lower court to deliver all of its information in a case so that a higher court may review it.

The U.S. Supreme Court ruled on both the statutory issue of racial discrimination in interstate commerce and held that Boynton had a federal right to remain in the white portion of the restaurant, as he was there "under authority of law."

The Freedom Riders

The Freedom Riders were a group of Black and white individuals who joined together to protest segregation in interstate travel. James "Jim" Farmer, was the National Director of the Congress of Racial Equality (CORE), when he became the "architect" of the original CORE Freedom Ride of 1961. Farmer believed that desegregating interstate travel was a way to garner media attention and effectively display the mission and goals of each trip. Some of the original Freedom Riders include Rep. John Lewis (TN), Stokley Carmichael (NY), Glenda Gaither Davis,Rabbi Israel "Si" Dresner (NJ), Genevieve Hughes (MD), and Pauline Knight-Ofusu (TN).[42]

When John Lewis was arrested in Mississippi for participating in a Freedom Ride at 19 years old, he had already been arrested five times.

Lewis became a well-known Freedom Rider serving as the Chairman of the Student Nonviolent Coordinating Committee (SNCC), which afforded him a speaking role in the 1963 March on Washington with Dr. King as well as the 1965 March from Selma to Montgomery.[43]

Stokely Carmichael, known for his role in the Black Power Movement spoke about the impact of the Freedom Rides in his posthumous book,"CORE would be sending an integrated team-black and white together, from the nation's capital to New Orleans on public transportation. That's all. Except, of course, that they would sit randomly on the buses in integrated pairs and in the stations they would use waiting room facilities casually, ignoring the white/colored signs. What could be more harmless... in any even marginally healthy society?"

Glenda Gaither Davis recalls being arrested for attempting to use the restroom. She was sentenced to jail for 60 days and received a $200 fine. Davis states, "Even though we came from many different places and we had many different cultures and many different home environments, in some ways we were very much unified because we had a common cause... we knew that we had taken a stand and that there was something better out there for us."[44]

Blacks and whites joined the Freedom Rides and the outspoken Rabbi Israel "Si" Dresner was later called the most arrested rabbi in history and he participated in an Interfaith Freedom Ride from Washington, DC to Tallahassee, Florida, and continued to fight for civil rights until his retirement decades later. Another non-Black participant in the early Freedom Rides was CORE Field Secretary Genevieve Hughes from Maryland. In an interview, Hughes stated, "I figured Southern women should be represented so the South and the nation would realize all Southern people don't think alike."[45]

Pauline Knight-Ofusu was part of the Nashville Student Movement, and was arrested as a 20-year-old Tennessee State student in Jackson, Mississippi for participating in the Freedom Rides. She also led a brief hunger strike in jail. Pauline stated,"I got up one morning in May and I said to my folks at home, 'I won't be back today because I am a Freedom Rider. It was like a wave or a wind, and you didn't know where it was coming from but you knew you were supposed to be there. Nobody asked me, nobody told me."[46]

Reading the stories of the Freedom Riders and other young people who stood up against racism back then is mind-boggling. These heroes and sheroes risked their lives on the front line so that generations could be treated with fairness and dignity. We all owe the civil rights activists and pioneers our deepest gratitude.

Good Company

Researching the legacy of these other civil rights champions whom my father was in the same company lead me to believe that had he lived longer, he would have made strides for African Americans and achieved personal success like his counterparts. For example, Jack Greenberg, a Jewish lawyer and scholar, credits Thurgood Marshall as his mentor, served as Director Counsel for the NAACP Legal Defense Fund from 1961-1984, succeeding Marshall. Greenberg argued over 40 historic civil rights cases in the U.S. Supreme Court including *Brown v. Board of Education* and won the majority of them. He was also a professor at Columbia Law School and the Dean of Columbia College. Greenberg died in 2016 at the age of 91.[47]

Louis H. Pollak of Philadelphia, also argued several civil rights cases including *Brown v. Board of Education*. He attended Harvard and Yale and served as the Dean of the University of Pennsylvania Law School from 1975-1978 before being appointed to federal judge. Judge Pollak died of heart disease in 2012 at the age of 89.[48] Constance Baker Motley was a civil rights strategist and went on to become the first African American woman elected to the New York Senate in 1964, and then Manhattan Borough President in 1965. Later in 1966, President Lyndon B. Johnson named her as the first woman and first African American Federal Judge. She died in 2005 at the age of 84.[49]

Finally, there is not much I can write about Thurgood Marshall that has not already been written. He was a true warrior for segregation and civil rights. Marshall graduated *first* in his class from Howard University School of Law under the tutelage of Dean Hamilton Houston who was also dean when my father attended. Marshall became a lawyer for the NAACP and was recognized throughout the country for his civil rights victories. He argued 32 cases before the U.S. Supreme court and won 29. To date, no one has such a record. In 1961 President Kennedy appointed him to the U.S. Court of Appeals. A few years later President Johnson named Marshall as the first Black Solicitor General. Then in 1967, he became the first African American Supreme Court Justice appointed by President Johnson. For 24 years Marshall passionately defended the civil rights of minorities. [50] Justice Marshall died in 1993 at the age of 85.

CHAPTER 14

THE PETERSBURG 11

William R. McKenney Public Library

"If not us, who? If not now, when?"

- John F. Kennedy

T he time had come for Blacks in Richmond to stand up for desegregation of public facilities once and for all. How could they ever get ahead without education? Blacks gathered regularly at the Petersburg Public Library to study and increase their knowledge to make an impact in their communities. The Petersburg sit-in, led by Rev. Wyatt Tee Walker and Rev. R.G. Williams, was the first library sit-in around the country. It was the impetus of other public protests and sit-ins which led to Richmond's desegregation. My father was directly involved in this cause as was quoted on several occasions that he was prepared to take this case to the U.S. Supreme Court.

There were three library sit-ins in Petersburg and the first one was on Feb. 27, 1960. Rev. Walker approached the first floor counter and asked for a biography of Confederate hero Gen. Robert E. Lee. Only whites were allowed on the first floor and Blacks were only allowed in the basement. Walker's act led to a nine-month fight to integrate the library and the arrest of 11 people, including Walker and Williams, college students from Virginia State College and three Peabody High School students.

"The inability of African-Americans to use more than the basement of the library was "humiliating, embarrassing, unfair, nauseating, and unconstitutional."
- Clarence W. Newsome

As a result of the arrests, a meeting was held at the Zion Baptist Church where 1,400 people showed up in 27 degree weather. My father spoke to the people and assured those in attendance that he was filing an injunction and that segregation of this nature was unconstitutional. During that mass community meeting my father mentioned to the attendees that he received a telegram of encouragement and congratulations from Rev. Martin Luther King, Jr.[51]

A few days after that meeting, my father was ready to file the injunction with the Federal District Court in Richmond. He was accompanied on a 25 mile drive in a 30 car motorcade along with a police escort to file his motion on behalf of those arrested. An injunction is a court order which stops a person or organization from starting or continuing an action that threatens another's legal rights. In his statement to support his motion, he said, "the refusal of a city to make publicly supported facilities available on a nonsegregated basis to Negro citizens deprives them of Equal Protection of the laws."[52] The injunction was granted and that victory led to the desegregation of *all* public facilities in the city of Richmond.[53]

Again, my father worked hand-in-hand with some of the greatest civil rights pioneers of the era. The Petersburg Library was the first of 17 arrests of the late Rev. Dr. Wyatt Tee Walker, a prominent civil rights leader, minister, scholar and composer of Black gospel music. Dr. Walker was a minister at Gillfield Baptist Church in Petersburg but left to become the executive director of the Southern Christian Leadership Conference (SCLC), where he worked alongside Dr. Martin Luther King, Jr., his seminary friend while at VUU.[54]

"...the African American Organizations weren't sold on Newsome, although he was associated with Hill's law firm. They thought he was too outspoken."

- L. **Douglas Wilder***, Virginia's Native Son, commenting on his role as Clarence Newsome's Campaign Chair during Newsome's run for Richmond City Council in 1962*

CHAPTER 15

A RUN FOR CHANGE

---

*"It's only fair play to elect a Negro council so
that a minority group would be represented there."*

- **Clarence W. Newsome**

F
ighting to end segregation and other injustices armed
with the law, was my father's primary contribution to
the Civil Rights Movement in Virginia. So because of
his outspokenness, courtroom success, and passion for justice,
he had been urged by parts of the community to become a candidate for Richmond's City Council in 1962. Running for local
office was another way to make a greater impact for equality in
the community.

However, he had an uphill battle. There were 25 candidates
on the ballot and he was the only independent. He was one of
six candidates that the Crusade for Voters endorsed. Therefore,
the Black vote was split six ways which, L. Douglas Wilder, my
father's campaign chair, is quoted as saying, "You're killing him!"
Apparently, Wilder was disappointed that Black voters did not
unify their vote for the best candidate. The headlines for the

Richmond Times Dispatch stated, "25 Candidates: Campaign is thicket of contradictions and uncertainties.[55]

As the campaign chair, L. Douglass Wilder spoke of the climate during my father's run for office in his book, *Virginia's Native Son*.

> "I knew it was time for African Americans to start winning elections, but I was disenfranchised with the organizations that were setting up and endorsing candidates. Our community didn't know its own mind. Case in point: A prominent lawyer and community leader Clarence Newsome planned to run for city council. He came to me for help and I was glad to give it. I liked Newsome, and I thought he'd be the perfect candidate. We still hadn't broken the color barrier in the city council..."[56]

My father was also concerned about the next generation of Richmond's leaders. Not only was he the executive secretary of the Crusade for Voters but he was Chairman of the Committee Against Juvenile Delinquency, and the Secretary for the NAACP Redress Committee. Among his campaign promises was the implementation of a compulsory school attendance law. He also urged to end discrimination in city employment and desired to eradicate the lack of fair practices and promotions for government employees.

Although he had lost a few cases, I can't imagine how he felt losing his seat on Richmond's City Council. Not only did he lose, but he lost badly, coming in 10th out of the nine available seats. If there is any solace in his defeat, my father had the highest votes of any of the other five Black candidates. Losing the seat was probably a blow to his ego, yet he had several cases in the works both in court and out of court, so he had to shift gears and move on.

I have a photo of him in *Jet* handing Linwood Spencer, a railroad worker, a settlement check from the Norfolk & Western Railroad for $70,000 for his injuries on the job. My father preferred to settle as many cases as he could because the legal system was long and drawn-out. He had so many other legal victories in his short nine-year legal career.

A photo taken on a train ride during my father's campaign run for Richmond City Council. Clarence Newsome is standing in the background. L. Douglas Wilder is seated in the foreground, 1962.

PART III

FULL CIRCLE

CHAPTER 16

DNA

---

*"In all of us there is a hunger, marrow deep,
to know our heritage - to know who we are and
where we came from. Without this enriching knowledge, there is a hollow yearning. No matter what our
attainments in life, there is still a vacuum, an emptiness,
and the most disquieting loneliness."*

- Alex Haley

My dad died of renal failure secondary to hypertension, the silent killer. There were no public health
campaigns during that time and hypertension
ravaged the Black community. Like my father, I was diagnosed
with early onset hypertension at 28-years old. It wasn't until
I was in a car accident where I broke and dislocated my right
leg and ankle, that paternity reared its head. While in the hospital, my doctor noticed that my blood pressure could not be
regulated. At first she dismissed it as my anxiety over the car
accident and I was concerned that missing work would impact
my recently acquired employment with the Orange New Jersey

Public Schools. Yet as she continued to monitor my blood pressure, the numbers remained high. I told her what I knew about my family history on both sides. It became clear that I needed blood pressure medication.

By this time, I was seeing a great therapist to help me sort out my insatiable desire to connect with my dad, and other personal relationship challenges. While talking to my therapist I was still repeating my mother's narrative that my father drank himself to death and had kidney failure. He challenged the narrative by saying that if it were alcohol abuse that killed him, surely he would have shown liver problems, not kidney failure. *Why didn't I ever think of that?* I questioned myself a few times before I had the nerve to broach the subject of my father's death with my mother. *Was she hiding something from me?*

I called and told her that I wanted to speak with her about my father's death. I asked if she could provide me with his death certificate. She and daddy Duncan calmly sat nearby in the living room as I read the death certificate for the first time. That's when I read that my father had early onset hypertension and that it had indeed become a silent killer. He passed away at the age of 36, May 24, 1963, at 1:20 AM in Enion G. Williams Hospital. Although he was in the segregated portion of the hospital, I read an article which stated that the Black side of the hospital was held to high standards.[57]

I sat on the living room floor frozen. After quietly reading the death certificate, I alerted them that my blood pressure reading had been abnormal since my car accident. I was scheduled to see a specialist for more answers. When the results came in, I was diagnosed with an enlarged heart and early signs of kidney disease. I was afraid that I was now connected to my birth father in a bad way. I feared that I would never see the age of 36. This frightened my mother and she was moved to tears because as a young child, I used to tell her I did not think I was going to live long. For some reason, that was one comment that she let me know my father used to say. She found herself facing the nature versus nurture argument firsthand which she learned in sociology. There was a body of research at odds over which factor had the most influence on raising children: genetic or environment. I think she favored the idea of nurture, but this medical information was a jolt to that point of view.

There were times when my mother's untimely remarks were positive in tone. I was a "workaholic" which at the time when the word became trendy meant that I was hardworking, like my birth father. I was creative like he was and had an entrepreneurial spirit. He has been described in numerous articles as outspoken and radical, expressive using his hands with and dashingly handsome dimples. Once I was caught wringing my hands and my mother said, "Your Father used to do that and there's no way you would know that!" I was happy to hear her say these types of things, but I also knew that my father was somewhat anxious and always thinking about his next move. Yet my mother described him as being calm and not liking to argue. She said when she would get upset he would just look at her, refusing to jump in.

Goose Skin

Sadly, I recall my mother saying in frustration that I had skin like my father. The more I scrubbed my tusk-like skin on my elbows and knees, the more visible the bumps became. Mom also scolded me a few times because my lips were dark and accused me of being a smoker, which was not true. I adamantly denied her accusations as my dark lips are an attribute of my father.

My father and I have Keratosis pilaris (KP). Many other relatives that I connected with have the same issue. KP is a common inherited disorder of follicular hyperkeratosis. It has a stippled appearance on the skin resembling gooseflesh. The disorder most commonly affects the upper arms, upper legs, and buttocks. Patients with KP usually have no symptoms except complaints of visible appearance of bumps and dryness. Treatment options vary but the most important factor is to avoid dry skin, and use creams and topical steroids when necessary.

Fill in the Blanks

"Not everything that is faced can be changed,
but nothing can be changed until it is faced."
- James Baldwin

Most of us are familiar with a family tree which is a diagram that shows the names and relationships of generations of family members. During my early training as a clinical social worker, I was asked to do a family genogram. A genogram is also a graphic representation of the family, but it involves more detailed, personal information about each individual. Therapists use them to analyze and pinpoint hereditary patterns and psychological factors in family relationships.

While completing my genogram, it was somewhat embarrassing that I couldn't trace my roots back very far compared to my cohorts. They all had stories to share of their fathers. I had the stories from my cousin Kim, but many of which I couldn't verify, so I accepted her narrative. The ironic thing is that my mother and grandmother told me that my father was an alcoholic who drank himself to death. That characterization of him was part of the reason it became my mission to become a drug and alcohol prevention counselor. I wanted to save other children from having to go through this hurtful experience. So there I was in my training and still not able to answer critical questions about my past. At that time, I had no idea of my father's significant achievements for civil rights. I completed the genogram with what I knew about my mother's family history and indicated that my father was an alcoholic. Just writing the word "alcoholic" to describe my father makes me feel ashamed of myself. *Sorry daddy Newsome.* After finding out the truth about my father, one thing is for sure, Father's Day has never been the same.

CHAPTER 17

A YEAR OF TRAGEDY

"Until justice is blind to color,
until education is unaware of race,
until opportunity is unconcerned with
the color of men's skin, emancipation
will be a proclamation but not a fact.
- Lyndon B. Johnson

The year 1963 was indeed a tragic year in the Civil Rights Era. The assassination of key leaders in advancing civil rights of African Americans, such as President John F. Kennedy, Medgar Evers, the death of Attorney Martin A. Martin, and my father Clarence W. Newsome. My father's colleague and friend, Martin A. Martin, died two weeks before my father of a heart attack in his home.

When President Kennedy was assassinated the principal came to each classroom to make the announcement. As a result, schools were closed for half the day. When I was picked up from school and got home, my mother and grandmother were glued to the small black and white television. Reports of the assassination were steadily coming in. My mother and grand-mother were weeping. I tried my best to cry. It was a fake cry because I had no real knowledge of President Kennedy. I recall seeing his photo and he appeared young and handsome. My mother saw me and quickly scolded me, "Stop the noise Clare, you didn't even know who he was!" On cue, I stopped my acting performance.

No Goodbyes

Prior to my father's death, he sent a letter to my uncle James, asking to see Sheila and me. He encouraged us to come quickly due to his medical condition. I remember when uncle James came next door and was speaking with my mother about the letter. She went to the small drawer on the side table and hand-ed him a studio portrait photograph of Sheila and me. Uncle James sent the photos off. The thought that my father died wanting to see us on his deathbed and we were not allowed to go is unbearable.

On May 29, 1963, Nana answered the phone and alert-ed my mother that someone was on the phone for her. It was my father's second wife. She told my mother that Clarence had passed, the funeral was over, and that he had been cremated. I remember my mother squealed in a piercing wail that I will nev-er forget. My grandmother came running to her side. As they closed the pocket doors to the bedroom their voices became muffled. When they emerged, they told us that our father was dead.

What is dead? I asked.

"Your father is not alive anymore. You will never see him," my mom responded.

Just then I heard daddy Duncan's keys open the front door. I ran to the door.

"He's not dead mommy!"

My maternal Nana proceeded to say as she walked back to the kitchen, "That's not your real father!" At six years old I was more confused on that day than ever before. It seemed like the anger was ricocheting off the walls. My mother was angry at what my Nana said. She was angry at the news she had received from the other Mrs. Newsome. There was bad blood between Mrs. Newsome #1 and Mrs. Newsome #2. Always one to speak up, I asked my mom what did cremation mean. She insensitively blurted out, "She burned the man up! Your father is dead!" My sister remembers yelling "Yay" and I being younger, followed her lead. My mother was furious at our reaction.

I was shocked and frightened by my mother's statement. *Why would they burn up a dead man?* I thought. *Had he done something bad?* I became angry with this second wife but I had no place to express my anger. I simply buried it deep within me. I felt like she had done something unfair to my mother, Sheila, and me. It wasn't until years later that I realized Mrs. Newsome #2 lied about the cremation. *Why would she do such a hurtful thing?*

Daddy Duncan came home everyday from General Motors at four PM like clockwork. We usually ran to the door to give him a hug and he always told us not to touch him until he got cleaned up. Sheila and I loved the strong scent of Aqua Velva once he came out of the bathroom. But on this day, he heard my mother crying in the bedroom. He was disturbed to find his wife crying. He asked her what was wrong and she told him about my father. I do not remember if he was tender towards her at first but he certainly was irritated at her level of grief. I remember him storming out after asking her "Are you still in love with this man?" Mom tried to justify her tears as she pointed toward my sister and me. "I have his children," she said. He retorted with one of his typical phrases, "Well I be damned!"

This is a day I will never forget because my daddy Duncan had a temper like an inferno or volcanic eruption. He never lashed out at us or our mom, but we have seen him in action a number of times with others. I remember thinking that it was not a good idea for mom to be talking about this Clarence fellow. Daddy Duncan was about to leave the house but not without sending my Nana home. My Nana looked sad and kept her eyes toward the floor as she left. She took her portion of the dinner she cooked wrapped inside a plastic bag and went out the side door. My sister and I were sent to our room. The house was eerily quiet for the rest of that evening.

I don't think parents realize that the walls have ears and children are listening. Even when they use big words and think kids don't understand, the tone and other words give enough context for kids to put two and two together, as the old folks used to say.

I'm not sure if my father knew for certain that he was dying until the end. Why didn't my mother allow us to see him? Maybe she didn't believe him? How could she have known that he only had three weeks to live? Maybe she didn't want us to see him in such a fragile state? My mind races with so many questions that I will never have answers. Yet, I am comforted by the fact that he received good care when he entered the Enion G Williams hospital in Richmond.[58] I spoke with my cousin Kim about my father's final days. She told me that his mother and sisters were with him in the hospital the entire time. Her words helped dislodge some of my grief and brought me peace of mind.

After all his legal victories in the south as a civil rights attorney, malignant hypertension had taken a deadly toll. There was no dialysis or kidney transplants done in the U.S. at that time. Several days later, I heard a very shocking outburst from my mother. After opening the mail she held a paper and said "They didn't even list his children in the obituary!" Her frustration about the obituary never seemed to end. In hindsight, knowing that my father loved us and was willing to take care of us leads me to believe that he never mentioned us for our own safety, as with other children of The Movement.

May 24 1963, after just 22 days in the hospital, my father succumbed to renal failure at 1:20 A.M. Sheila and I never got a chance to say goodbye. Thank you daddy Newsome for leaving such an indelible legacy for our family, for America, and for Black people.

Goodbye daddy Newsome, you will forever hold a place in my heart and be sorely missed. Image of my father's estate.

INVENTORY OF ESTATE OF

CLARENCE W. NEWSOME, Deceased

Central National Bank - checking account	
First Federal Savings & Loan Co. - Savings acct.	576.70
	3,010.41
Richmond Teachers Credit Union - deposit	5.21
Accounts Receivables	2,169.50
1963 Lincoln Automobile	4,600.00
Office Furniture and Law Books	510.00
Interest on savings account	110.82
Total	10,982.64

N.B. The following have not yet been converted to cash:

Accounts Receivable -------------	2,000.00	
Office Furniture, etc.	445.00	2,445.00
Actual cash received -----------		8,537.64
Disbursements to 12/5/63........		3,206.98
Balance cash 12/5/63------------		4,830.66

Image of my father's death certificate.

CHAPTER 18

MIRROR, MIRROR

"As I reflect on my father's accomplishments,
I see his reflection in my sister and me."

Duing my early years of Family Therapy training a two-way mirror was an effective tool used to train therapists. This technique allowed for the therapist and the family to benefit from multiple therapists behind the mirror to observe the client/therapist encounter from a neutral point of view. It was also designed to make observations relevant to the supervision necessary for the therapist to hone their craft. At times, the phone would ring and therapists behind the mirror would call in and suggest a question or ask family members to change seats to test out different family dynamics. The shrouded therapy session involved a staff that held high trust of senior staff that they could one day hope to become.

When I think of my father, I think of him as a lawyer-activist. I see myself as a social work advocate, therapist, educator, administrator, and preacher. My sister inherited the protest gene and she expressed it throughout her high school and college years. She led that movement into the classroom and advocated for Special Needs children. Later, she led that protest to Boston University as she became the first Black woman to be named Dean of the Boston University School of Theology. At present, she gives life and hope as a full-time pastor. I think Sheila and I are examples of daddy Newsome's platform, to" accelerate on all fronts."

In my career, I also addressed the marginalized and disenfranchised populations to challenge the system and treat them fairly. My father's "Lets Play Fair" platform slogan for his Richmond Council run included his concerns about equal pay, truancy policies, desegregation of libraries, restaurants, retail stores, and buses. He wanted equal wages and more jobs to be created for Black people. He challenged the people who sat under his voice to be action-oriented and to rise up against discrimination and injustices. He was articulate, well-dressed, and prepared. He answered the call of his generation with boldness, intellect, and action. During a visit to Richmond, I stopped by a barber shop and asked if anyone remembered his name. The response was a pleasant surprise. He is still remembered today in his old neighborhood as a man of the people. I'm proud to place his name in print once again as a historical figure during the Civil Rights Era.

My fight originated in the inner City of Baltimore's urban medical clinics. Thousands of residents were frail, without insurance, and living in poverty. Many needed multiple levels of assistance. This included initiating them into the appropriate systems, and insurance companies who made accessing their benefits a chore of madness. I manned 24-hour call lines helping residents make it through the night until the sun came up. I showed up for them in the therapy room and in the classroom.

In my career in education and mental health the similarities to my father's work is embedded in the systems of care and how they operate. Where there is institutional racism, there is a breakdown in the system. Access is not denied by color per se, but trust in the healthcare system remains a problem. Early diagnosis and prevention are critical for the Black community to lead longer, healthier lives.

I've been in many counseling sessions of underserved populations of adolescents attending school with manifestations of urban social ills. Many were angry and self- medicating on illegal drugs. Others were parenting their younger siblings due to the incarceration of their parents, death of parents from heroin or the crack cocaine epidemic. Part of my work as a counselor, and later administrator, was to fight for their minds and their rights to be educated. Many students faced emotional upheavals moving from place to place while trying to work to feed themselves. There were thousands more battling organic issues and learning disabilities.

Many times, fighting for students meant fighting against the very system I worked for. For example, the laws and policies of the truancy office clashed with the dropout policies. The Juvenile Court System had another set of policies that were often in conflict with students' rights for treatment if they were drug or alcohol dependent. In instances where confidentiality was at issue, federal medical records laws were at odds with the discipline policy. There were students who were emancipated and living on their own but failed to meet residency requirements.

I fought to teach students the skills needed to resist negative peer pressure while skill building with them on the negative biological effects drugs and alcohol and other substances have on their development. Exposure to unwanted pregnancies, HIV/AIDS, STD's and more needed to be addressed just to keep this fragile population in school on time or be marked absent.

Like the early legal pay for civil rights lawyers, the helping professions only receive average pay, but the wins are priceless. I believe that my sister and I are on the other side of the mirror. As a matter of fact, our mother's lifelong social work career to this same underserved population and missionary work with the women in the church complement the work my sister and I feel led to continue. It is as if the generation before us downloaded their intentions into our identities. Many traits of my parents such as critical thinking and analysis, creativity, musical gifts, and a heart to help others is innate.

I imagine the complexities of being a lawyer, researching cases, and building a strong argument of defense took a toll on my father's health. The long hours required to write a brief and prepare for court, as well as the continuous pace of the work, made him the target of poor health habits and common chronic

diseases. Both my father and I were driven to make a differ-
ence, to remove pain and suffering to the best of our ability. I
share the love of research and Black history and I hope this story
challenges us to look deeply into how the Movement became
everyone's movement.

EPILOGUE

The more things change, the more they remain the same...

In 1968 when Dr. King was assassinated I was looking at my small black and white RCA television in my room. I was shocked at the level of chaos, violence, and people running through the streets. The fires across the screen made my heart beat faster. My mother came into my room and told me to turn the TV off for the rest of the night. I was scared. I was confused. This incident seemed close to home. Daddy Duncan told me the streets were blocked and people could not get into Newark to our church. At some point, daddy said he was going to go and see for himself. The panic in my home rose to a new level of fervor as everyone was afraid he would go out the front door and not come back. I had no real appreciation of the work of Dr. King. I was clear that he was a Black man trying to do good for the Black people. My mother was raising us in a bicultural world where being Black was not something bad. We were in multicultural circles as she broke the color barriers in her profession. I did not see myself as different or Black or nonwhite. I was simply Clarencia, my mom's daughter. I could not understand the revolution or why people were so angry. As I matured, and attended a HBCU I saw more and more racial events unfold. Although I was not as "woke" as my sister Sheila, I saw firsthand the blatant inequalities in the inner city educational system, employment, social services, and healthcare.

Health disparities continue to abound in America between whites and non –whites. Black women are more likely to die during or after childbirth. These issues are well-documented today and while The Civil Rights Movement is being celebrated for crossing over the fifty year mark there is so much more work to be done. Celebrating the milestone is important, but balancing the scorecard should be a priority. The question remains is are we better off now than we were in the 1960's? Have we been able to sustain the progress of the Black activists before us?

Answers to these questions have been researched by the Kerner Commission and compiled in a report in 2018. In 1968, the National Advisory Commission on Civil Disorders, presented a report to President Johnson to examine the causes of civil unrest in African American communities.[59] The report found that "white racism" lead to employment discrimination, and discrimination in education and housing, were the leading factors to economic disparities. The authors of the report urged the President to commit to common opportunities for all people regardless of race. Fifty years later, the Kerner Report, states that, "While African Americans are in many ways better off in absolute terms than they were in 1968, they are still disadvantaged in important ways relative to whites. In several important respects, African Americans have actually lost ground relative to whites, and, in a few cases, even relative to African Americans in 1968.[60]

In reviewing the three key findings in the areas of education, employment and housing, a summary of the results revealed that Blacks are better educated than in 1968, yet still fall behind whites in overall attainment. I believe my father would be pleased in the area but of course he would urge Blacks to do better. With regard to wages, Black wages are higher than in the past, yet Black workers make 82.5 cents on every dollar earned by whites. Sadly, Blacks are 2.5 times more likely to live in poverty than whites. White family wealth is 10 times the wealth as the median Black family. The more dismal statistics can be seen in the areas of homeownership, unemployment, and incarceration. The report illustrates that "America has failed to deliver any progress for African Americans over the last five decades."[61] More importantly, "in 2015, the Black homeownership rate was just over 40 percent, virtually unchanged since 1968, and Blacks in prison or jail almost tripled between 1968 and 2016 and is currently more than six times the white incarceration rate."[62]

The same "white racism" that was the culprit to Black advancement in the 1968 Kerner Report is the same negative state of our current socio-political landscape. Certain civil rights laws and social services to minorities are being rolled back. We are experiencing the vitriol of the past in the post-Barack Obama presidency. The hateful rhetoric, violence, and resurgence of white supremacist propaganda along with Nationalism is eerily familiar to the days when my father and his brave legal colleagues did everything in their power to dismantle Jim Crow laws and fight for equality. There is a deepening divide in America and there is an even deeper division among Blacks. Are the deep divisions of thought from W.E.B Dubois and Marcus Garvey's ideologies appearing as far as the east is from the west re-emerging?

It seems as if America has lost its confidence in itself to hold on to one definition of democracy and justice for all. The deep divide of action steps from Malcolm X and Dr. King were blatant in the early Movement as well. Although everyone did not always agree on the strategy, they agreed on the target, and through the legal system, they won many battles. However, where is the dogma and strategy of today in the 21st Century? The Black Community is divided into self-inflicted segregationist ideas based on demographics of economic and educational strata. The Black community's outrage with police brutality and drug-addicted youth do not point to a single source. Blaming and finger-pointing at various contributors waters down our approaches to freedom and liberty today.

The population, both young and old, no longer trust the same institutions that outlawed Jim Crow. Not to mention that the term "civil rights" has taken on new meaning for other disenfranchised groups who are marginalized. My father seemed to be ahead of his time when he suggested that the Black community should accelerate on all fronts to change the tide. He was fiercely impatient with the one track model that appeared safer at the time. Strategically, it would have been better to have multiple approaches to defeat the common target. Some would argue that this approach could make the fight for freedom diluted by spreading our collective power too thin. We will never know the full extent of my father's plans to help alleviate the inequalities and injustices against Black people.

Women's rights, LGTBQ rights, are now considered the platforms for civil rights, while Black children still suffer disproportionate barriers to health, education, and fairness in the courts. Americans are exhausted, stressed, and deeply divided over the lack of a clear path to the American dream. Most people are working multiple jobs with low wages which has replaced quality family time. New terminology such as "democratic socialism" enter the crowded arena of labels that people identify themselves with politically. The country is in crisis and the Black community's fracture between saving our sons and daughters turns into endless episodic days and nights of the haves and have nots. We have to collectively work together to do more.

There are many ways to be outspoken today. President Barack Obama reminded the crowd in his 2016 Democratic convention speech to not "boo" but to vote. In 1960, when the 34 VUU students were arrested, my father spoke to over 600 people at the Cedar Street Memorial Baptist Church and advised them to "Use the ballot box, the economic boycott, and then go in, sit down, and eat." The boycotts were effective and after several months, restaurants and retailers in Richmond dismantled segregation in private establishments.

The early Civil Rights Movement could be summed up as fighting forward in the areas of human dignity and fairness, whereas the Black Lives Matter Movement can be summed up

as fighting against the resurgence of old behavior and thinking. It is a movement of ideologies. The current Movement is
not supported by any particular organization. Unlike the Civil
Rights Movement which was catapulted to center stage by the
Black Church, the lawyer-activists, the court system, and the
working class people who boycotted buses and stores, the current Movement needs more outspoken men like my father and
his colleagues. We all know better so it's up to us to do better. If
you are not in a position to use your voice and speak out against
Black injustices, then use your gifts and intellect to help others,
and change the socio-economic tide. The game hasn't changed
and the rules are the same. Not only should we seek to play fair,
but we must all play to win!

My son Leon and my granddaughter, and my father on the right.
Spitting images minus my father's dimple.

My daughter Sharm and her grandma Clara Newsome, displaying the beautiful Newsome eyes.

My sister Imani-Sheila and me, Christmas 2019.

The Newsome legacy continues…
Imani-Sheila and my niece Mariama Camara.

The Newsome-Shade family, Easter 2019.

ABOUT THE AUTHOR

D r. Clarencia R. Newsome-Shade, LCSW, M.Ed., Th.d, is an ordained minister and has worked extensively in education and healthcare. She is a psychotherapist in private practice and an organizational consultant offering employee assistance for businesses and Christian counseling. She empowers ministers to take care of their mental and emotional health so they can serve the people of God. Through seminars and workshops, she educates people about wellbeing and spiritual strength. She provides consultation for groups and leaders of churches so they can continue to guide churches. She makes frequent media appearances to offer her ministry. Rev.

Shade embraced Jesus Christ as Savior in her youth and received her first Missionary license in 1987 in the Churches of God in Christ. She has held multiple leadership positions including District Supervising Missionary. This appointment involves overseeing the ministry work of women in the New Garden State Jurisdiction, in the State of New Jersey.

Professionally, Dr. Shade formerly worked as the Director of Student Support Services as the head of a multimillion-dollar substance abuse prevention program for the public schools in Newark, New Jersey. She managed a staff of 300 with three supervisors from the Central Office. The grants oversight, budget and reporting to the U.S. Department of Education while maintaining the local budget was among her many responsibilities. She is certified as a Family Therapist, a Substance Abuse prevention specialist while earning a Master's in Educational Leadership (M.Ed.) and several other educational certifications.

In addition, she holds a dual MSW degree with a concentration in clinical and administrative social work. This qualifies her to provide clinical supervision to social workers to help them fulfill licensing requirements. She also qualifies as a Licensed Clinical Social Worker currently in private clinical practice. She has received and earned a Doctorate in Theology.

She uses all her gifts including singing. She has appeared off-Broadway, in the play *Faith Journey*. She has done studio work as a backup singer and recorded one gospel album. She now sings with the internationally Grammy award-winning choir, Rev. Stef and Jubilation Choir. Her favorite scripture is Proverbs 3:5,6.

Dr. Shade is the author of the book, *Conquering Soul Holes* and many articles.

She is the proud mother of two adult children and four grand-children.

Clarence W. Newsome Biographical Timeline and Civil Rights Movement Highlights	
1927	Clarence W. Newsome was born to Joseph Newsome and Clara Bell Hamm in Columbus, Ohio.
1933	Oliver Hill, graduated from Howard Law School second to Thurgood Marshall. Marshall formed his own practice as well at the NAACP Legal Defense and Education Fund. My father became a key player working with these two legal scholars after graduating from law school.
1939	Spottswood Robinson III graduated from Howard Law and received the highest average in the history of the law school. Robinson went on to be a premier lawyer with the NAACP Legal Defense fund working on hundreds of civil rights cases with Marshall, and a few with my father at the Hill firm.
1943	Attorney Martin A. Martin became the first African American attorney in the Criminal Trial Division of the U.S. Department of Justice. Years later, Martin worked closely with my father at the Hill law firm on hundreds of civil rights cases and he was the attorney of record for my parent's divorce.
1945	Newsome graduated from Lucy Addison High School in Roanoke, Virginia and enrolled in Virginia Union University.

1948	President Truman signed Executive Order 9980 which prohibited discrimination in civilian agencies and instituted fair employment practices and Executive Order 9981 which abolished racial discrimination in the armed forces.
1948	Oliver Hill formed the law firm Hill, Tucker and Robinson
1949	Newsome graduated from Virginia Union University.
1950	Newsome attended Howard University Law School in Washington, D.C.
1952	Newsome met Cora Jeffries (my mother) at Howard University and they eloped.
1953	Newsome graduated from Howard University Law School and passed the Virginia Bar. While at Howard he was active in the student activities of the NAACP under the encouragement of Dean Howard Houston who urged his law students to be "social engineers." Newsome had a clerkship with Belford V. Lawson.
1953	My sister Sheila Diane Newsome was born.
1954	*Brown v. Board of Education of Topeka, Kansas*, held that public education and segregation of children in public schools on the basis of race, deprived equal educational opportunities to children of the minority group. Thurgood Marshall argued this case and won. Marshall won more Supreme Court cases than any lawyer to date. He later became the first African American U.S. Supreme Court Justice.

1955	Emmett Till is brutally murdered for allegedly flirting with a white woman.
1955	Rosa Parks refuses to give up her seat to a white woman on a bus in Montgomery, Alabama.
1954-1956	Newsome was drafted as an officer in the U.S. Army and stationed inBerlin, Germany. He received an honorable discharge and the Medal of Good Conduct.
1956	Clarencia Rene Newsome was born.
1956	Governor Thomas B. Stanley announces a package of Massive Resistance legislation that became known as the Stanley Plan which gave him the power to close schools rather than desegregate.
1957	The Civil Rights Act of 1957 established the Civil Rights Commission to protect an individual's rights to equal protection and protected some civil and voting rights, but it lacked substantial enforcement mechanisms.
1957	Nine Black students sought attendance at Central High School in Little Rock Arkansas. They were denied entry by the National Guard and President Eisenhower sent federal troops to escort the students to school.
1958	Newsome became Chairman of the NAACP Redress Committee. Prior to that he was an attorney with the Legal Defense Fund, and held other NAACP roles including Secretary and head of the Education Fund. During that time my parents separated.

1959	My parents divorce was finalized.
1959	The Virginia Supreme Court of Appeals as well as the U.S. District Court rule that Massive Resistance to prevent desegregation is unconstitutional.
1960	My mother married Alfonso Duncan in East Orange, New Jersey
1960	My father married Thelma Kitty Gilpen in Richmond, Virginia
1960	Greensboro, North Carolina Woolworth sit-ins at "whites only" counter by four Black college students.
1960	My father presents the case on behalf of the Richmond 34 trespass arrest at Thalhimers Department store. He also presents the case of Boynton, the Freedom Rider. Both cases go all the way to the U.S. Supreme Court. My father died before he learned of his victory in the Richmond 34 case.
1960	Ruby Bridges, age 6, is escorted to school by armed federal marshals inLouisiana.
1961	Clarence Newsome files petition to desegregate the St. Petersburg Library after the arrest of Rev. Wyatt T. Walker and 10 individuals.

1962	Clarence Newsome runs for Richmond City Council with L.Douglas Wilder as his Campaign Chair. Newsome was unsuccessful, yet he had the most votes of the other five Black candidates. L. Douglas Wilder went on to become a Virginia Senator, the Mayor of Richmond and the first African American Governor of Virginia. That same year, my father also ran for President of the Richmond NAACP and lost by 70 votes.
1963	Clarence Newsome attends the funeral of colleague Martin A. Martin who died of a heart attack, at age 52.
May 24, 1963	Clarence Newsome dies after a three-week hospital stay due to renal failure and hypertension, at age 36.
1963	Dr. Martin Luther King Jr.'s March on Washington for Jobs and Freedom... *I Have a Dream Speech.*
1963	Four young girls are killed by the bombing of the 16th Street Baptist Church in Birmingham, Alabama.
1963	President John F. Kennedy is assassinated and Vice President Lyndon B. Johnson becomes President.
1964	The Civil Rights Act became the law which outlawed discrimination based on race, color, religion, sex, or national origin.

1965	Henry L. Marsh who worked with my father earlier in his career on desegregation cases and formed his own firm with Samuel Tucker. Marsh later joined Oliver Hill's firm and worked on more than 50 desegregation cases. Marsh became the first African American Mayor of Richmond and served in the Virginia Senate for many years.
1965	Malcolm X is assassinated at a rally in New York City.
1965	Hundreds of civil rights activists organized by Rep. John Lewis marched from Selma to Montgomery to protest voter suppression and they are beaten, attacked by police and the tragic incident became known as Bloody Sunday. This led to the passage of the Voting Rights Act signed by President Johnson granting Blacks the right to vote.
1968	Dr. Martin Luther King Jr is assassinated as well as Attorney General Robert F. Kennedy. Also, the Civil Rights Act Outlawing Housing Discrimination was signed into law.
1969-2020 and beyond	The fight for African American justice and equality continues.

For bookings and more information,
visit: www.outspokenlawyer.com

ENDNOTES

1. https://www.blueknot.org.au/Resources/Information/Understanding-abuse-and-trauma/What-is-childhood-trauma

2. https://www.styleweekly.com/richmond/closing-statement/Content?oid=1646015

3. The Baltimore Afro-American Newspaper September 6, 1958

4. Norfolk Journal and Guide, April 25, 1959, p. 9

5. The Baltimore Afro-American Newspaper March 19, 1960, p. 9

6. The Chicago Defender (National edition) April 2, 1960

7. Norfolk Journal & Guide, May 12, 1962

8. Nixon v. Herndon, 273 U.S. 536 (1927)

9. http://www.naacp.org/oldest-and-boldest/naacp-history-charles-harrison-houston

10. www.law.cornell.edu/houston/housbio.htm

11. Howard University Bison yearbook, 1953

12. https://www.ferris.edu/HTMLS/news/jimcrow/question/2016/november.htm

13. https://www.encyclopediavirginia.org/massive_resistance

14. August 3, 1957, ProQuest Historical Newspapers, The Baltimore Afro-American

15. Psychology Today article see also (Kelly 2009).

16. Ibid

17. Blake, John, *Children of the Movement: The Sons and Daughters of Martin Luther King, Jr., Malcolm X, Elijah Muhammad, George Wallace, Andrew Young, Julian Bond, Stokely Carmichael, Bob Moses, James Chaney, Elaine Brown, and Others Reveal How the Civil Rights Movement Tested and Transformed Their Families,* Lawrence Hill, Chicago, 2004.

18. https://www.researchgate.net/publication/265219516_ The_Role_of_Father_Involvement_in_the_Perceived_ Psychological_Well-Being_of_Young_Adult_Daughters_A_Retrospective_Study

19. https://www.smithsonianmag.com/science-nature/the-microscopic-structures-of-dried-human-tears-180947766/

20. Singleton, Theresa A., 'The archeology of Slavery in North America" Annual Review of Anthropology, Vol. 24, (1995), pp 119-140

21. https://www.nytimes.com/1994/07/22/theater/theater-review-the-early-civil-rights-movement-set-to-music.html

22. https://www.biography.com/news/lorraine-hansberry-raisin-in-the-sun-summary-black-history

23. Ibid

24. *Ebony,* March 1961, Volume 16, no5

25. Sadler & Whitehead Architects, PLC, Richmond, VA. Report prepared by Kathryn Colwell, James Hill, Susan Horner, Kathy Lucas, Mary Harding Sadler, June 17, 2002.

26. Case Western Reserve Law Review·Volume 67·Issue 4·2017 The Courage of Civil Rights Lawyers

27. New Journal and Guide April 4th 1960

28. https://www.styleweekly.com/richmond/the-barriers-they-broke/Content?oid=1368704

29. Randolph v. Commonwealth, 202 Va. 661 (1961)

30. https://www.styleweekly.com/richmond/the-barriers-they-broke/Content?oid=1368704

31. Hall Commonwealth, 188 Va. 72, 77, 49 S.E.2d 369, 371 (appeal dismissed 335 U.S. 875, 69 S. Ct. 240, 93 L.ed. 418), See also, Henderson Trailway Bus Company, D.C. Va., F.Supp. (decided March 24, 1961)

32. Section 18-225 of the Code of 1950 (as amended by Acts of 1956, ch. 587, p. 942; Acts of 1958, ch. 166, p. 218)

33. See State Clyburn, 247 N.C. 455, 101 S.E.2d 295; State Avent, 253 N.C. 580, 118 S.E.2d 47; Williams Howard Johnson's Restaurant, 4 Cir. 268 F.2d 845; Slack Atlantic White Tower System, Inc., D.C.Md., 181 F. Supp. 124, affirmed 4 Cir., 284 F.2d 746; Griffin Collins, D.C.Md., 187 F. Supp. 149; Wilimington Parking Authority Burton, Del. , 157 A.2d 894; Shelley Kraemer, 334 U.S. 1, 13, 68 S. Ct. 836, 842, 92 L. Ed. 1161, 3 A.L.R.2d 441; See Alpaugh Wolverton, 184 Va. 943, 36 S.E.2d 906.

34. Alpaugh Wolverton, 184 Va. 943, 36 S.E.2d 906, Annotation, 9 A.L.R. 379. See also, Annotation, 33 A.L.R. 421. To the same effect see Brookside-Pratt Mining Co. Booth, 211 Ala. 268, 100 So. 240, 33 A.L.R. 417.

35. https://www.styleweekly.com/richmond/the-barriers-they-broke/Content?oid=1368704

36. Ibid

37. Ibid

38. https://www.richmond.com/elizabeth-johnson-rice/article_82824457-1292-551d-9d0e-b74b85d40a36.html

39. thehistorymakers.org/biography/honorable-henry-l-marsh-iii

40. Boynton v. Virginia, 364 U.S. 454 (1960)

41. https://www.history.com/topics/black-history/freedom-rides

42. http://www.pbs.org/wgbh/americanexperience/features/meet-players-freedom-riders/

43. Ibid

44. Ibid

45. Ibid

46. Ibid

47. https://www.nytimes.com/2016/10/13/us/jack-greenberg-dead.html

48. https://www.law.upenn.edu/live/news/2068-hon-louis-pollak-constitutional-law-scholar-and

49. https://www.britannica.com/biography/Constance-Baker-Motley

50. https://www.history.com/topics/black-history/thurgood-marshall

51. March 19, 1960; Pro Quest Historical Newspapers: The Baltimore Afro-American

52. New Journal and Guide, April 4, 1960

53. https://www.progress-index.com/article/20100226/news/302269935

54. https://library.richmond.edu/collections/rare/walker.html

55. Richmond Times Dispatch, March 12, 1962

56. Wilder, L. Douglas, Virginia's Native Son: The Election and Administration of Governor L. Douglas Wilder, Purdue University Press, P. 55 (2000)

57. Shaye Ellis, *Medical Monopoly: Twentieth Century Expansion of MCV.*

58. Ibid

59. https://www.epi.org/publication/50-years-after-the-kerner-commission/

60. Ibid

61. Ibid

62. Ibid

Made in the USA
Middletown, DE
14 February 2020

84518534R00116